This book belongs to:

Matthew
Nathanael
Bethany
Andrew

Merry Christmas 1990 to all.
love from
Cherie and Bob

IMAGINARY GARDENS

Harry N. Abrams, Inc.,
Publishers, New York

WHAT VOICE AT MOTH-HOUR

Robert Penn Warren

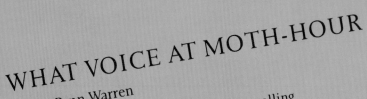

W hat voice at moth-hour did I hear calling
As I stood in the orchard while the white
Petals of apple blossoms were falling,
Whiter than moth-wing in that twilight?

What voice did I hear as I stood by the stream,
Bemused in the murmurous wisdom there uttered,
While ripples at stone, in their steely gleam,
Caught last light before it was shuttered?

What voice did I hear as I wandered alone
In a premature night of cedar, beech, oak,
Each foot set soft, then still as stone
Standing to wait while the first owl spoke?

The voice that I heard once at dew-fall, I now
Can hear by a simple trick. If I close
My eyes, in that dusk I again know
The feel of damp grass between bare toes,

Can see the last zigzag, sky-skittering, high,
Of a bullbat, and even hear, far off, from
Swamp-cover, the whip-o-will, and as I
Once heard, hear the voice: *It's late! Come home.*

The Garden
by David Hockney, 1980

Imaginary Gardens

American Poetry and Art for Young People

edited by Charles Sullivan

This book is dedicated to my son

JOHN SULLIVAN

who taught me how to see
the houseboat and the mouse
and other things

Editor:
LOIS BROWN

Designer:
CAROL ANN ROBSON

Rights and Reproductions:
FREDERIC ROY

Library of Congress Cataloging-in-Publication Data

Imaginary gardens : American poetry and art for young people / edited
   by Charles Sullivan.
        p.   cm.
      Includes index.
      Summary: Includes a selection of poems by American poets and works
of art by a variety of artists.
      ISBN 0-8109-1130-2
      1. Young adult poetry, American.   2. Children's poetry, American.
[1. American poetry—Collections.   2. Art appreciation.]
I. Sullivan, Charles,   1933-   .
PS586.3.I43 1989
700'.973—dc19   89-271

A Times Mirror Company

Printed and bound in Hong Kong

TO THE READER

I bought my son a *Talking Heads* tape for his birthday, this year, and I played some of it before I wrapped it up to mail to him. I didn't understand very much—the music was loud, the words hard to hear, hard for me to understand. Then I discovered a little booklet in the tape box, which contained the lyrics to each of the songs. I tried reading them while the tape was playing, and this helped a little. I tried reading them while the tape was *not* playing, and this helped a lot. Suddenly I could understand what the song "Ruby Dear" was all about:

> 'Round and 'round and we won't let go
> And where we stop no one knows
> Uh-huh
> Uh-huh
> Down and down in a spin we turn
> Looking like we'll never learn
> Uh-huh
> Uh-huh
> Think about what ev'ryone is saying
> Ruby dear
> Oh don't you hear
> Late at night when the radio is playing
> Ruby dear
> So looky here
> Oh, this record's broken . . . .

This isn't just noise, I said to myself, this is poetry. I can understand the words of it, and I can feel the feelings, too—sometimes I get so confused that I'm spinning like a broken record, moving around but getting nowhere fast. You may be a lot younger than I, but you have probably felt this also. And your parents—have they ever felt it? I doubt if there is much of a generation gap in basic human feelings. But when I turn the tape back on, there's a difference between us. You (like my son) can still hear the words and understand them and relate to them. I (like your parents) may be baffled by the music, by the "noise."

So it's easier for you to understand poetry—which is usually words without music—than it is for older people to understand rock. You don't think so? Try this:

> maggie and milly and molly and may
> went down to the beach (to play one day)
>
> and maggie discovered a shell that sang
> so sweetly she couldn't remember her troubles, and
> milly befriended a stranded star
> whose rays five languid fingers were;
>
> and molly was chased by a horrible thing
> which raced sideways while blowing bubbles: and
>
> may came home with a smooth round stone
> as small as a world and as large as alone.
>
> For whatever we lose (like a you or a me)
> it's always ourselves we find in the sea.

You've seen shells, starfish, crabs, stones. You know what it's like to be alone—how small you feel, compared to that bigness. And if you've ever stood or walked quietly on the beach, just you, paying attention to nothing else but the sea, you don't need me to explain what the last line of this poem means.

But a lot of poetry isn't like that, you say? A lot of it is old and hard to understand and *boring*, you think? I think so, too. But this doesn't mean that all poetry is bad; it means that we need to be selective, to pick out what is good from what isn't—just as we do with movies, clothes, teachers, or friends. Or rock music. "Good" means what is good for you; somebody else may like something that you dislike. And that's all right.

What I like best is the kind of poem that talks about something very real and true to me. It may be silly or serious; it may be old-fashioned or new; it may be written in simple words or it may take me a while to understand. But it has to be believable. As one poet said, we want to see "imaginary gardens with real toads in them." We can imagine almost anything a poet asks us to—a garden or a beach or a broken record spinning on a turntable—if it touches our feelings in a way that we know is true.

The poems in this book are about many different things—including a garden, a beach, a record, but also including pets and families, war, sports, outer space, living in a shoe—silly things and serious things that get all mixed together in this wonderful, scary adventure that we call "life."

Combined with the poetry are pictures of things that the poets were writing about. For example, with my poem, "Houseboat Mouse," you'll see a little drawing of a mouse dancing, like the one in the poem; you'll also find a painting of a houseboat— the wooden kind that some people lived on in years gone by. If my poem is a good poem, then you don't *need* these pictures to make the mouse and the houseboat real for you—your own imagination can do that. But the pictures may help you to see what I was looking at (or perhaps imagining) when I wrote this poem:

My house is a boat,
my boat is a house,
I live on the river
with Morris the mouse . . . .

Did this ever really happen? Who knows? It's happening now, in your imagination (and in mine). You'll just have to keep on wondering if I ever lived on a houseboat, or any kind of a boat, with or without a mouse.

This book has no rules. You don't have to read it if you don't want to. If you do want to read it, you can start anywhere you like—at the beginning, at the end, or in the middle. You can read one poem, or several, or all of them. You can sleep with this book under your pillow, or hide it in the wastebasket and hope that it will get thrown out with the trash. You are the boss of this book!

Naturally (being a parent) I hope that you won't throw the book away; somebody had to work hard to get it for you, and I and other people had to work hard to put it together. But a gift is not truly a gift if it has any "shoulds" tied to it. So what you do with this gift is up to you.

In fact, what you do with poetry is up to you. I hope you learn to enjoy it, but I would bite my tongue rather than say that you *should* enjoy it. That's your decision.

I will ask a favor of you, however. Please write and tell me how you like this book. Even if you don't like some of it (or all of it) I am interested in your opinions. Here's my name and address. (Do you think it's real?)

Charles Sullivan
Houseboat *Passages*
P. O. Box 1775
Annapolis, Maryland 21404

Carnation, Lily, Lily, Rose
John Singer Sargent, 1885–86

THERE ARE DIFFERENT GARDENS

Carl Sandburg

Flowers can be cousins of the stars.
The closing and speaking lips of the lily
And the warning of the fire and the dust—
They are in the gardens and the sky of stars.
Beyond the shots of the light of this sun
Are the little sprinkles, the little twinklers
Of suns to whose lips this lily never sent
A whisper from its closing and speaking lips.

POETRY

Marianne Moore

I too, dislike it: there are things that are important
    beyond all this fiddle.
Reading it, however, with a perfect contempt for it, one
    discovers that there is in
it after all, a place for the genuine.
    Hands that can grasp, eyes
      that can dilate, hair that can rise
        if it must, these things are important not because a

high sounding interpretation can be put upon them but
    because they are
useful; when they become so derivative as to become
unintelligible,
    the same thing may be said for all of us, that we
      do not admire what
      we cannot understand: the bat,
        holding on upside down or in quest of something to

eat, elephants pushing, a wild horse taking a roll, a tireless
        wolf under
    a tree, the immovable critic twitching his skin like a horse
        that feels a flea, the base-
    ball fan, the statistician—
      nor is it valid
        to discriminate against "business documents and

school-books"; all these phenomena are important. One must
        make a distinction
    however: when dragged into prominence by half poets, the
        result is not poetry,
    nor till the poets among us can be
      "literalists of
      the imagination"—above
        insolence and triviality and can present

for inspection, imaginary gardens with real toads in them,
        shall we have
    it. In the meantime, if you demand on one hand,
    the raw material of poetry in
      all its rawness and
      that which is on the other hand
        genuine, then you are interested in poetry.

The Horse
by Alexander Calder, 1976

A GIGANTIC BEAUTY OF A STALLION

from *Song of Myself*

Walt Whitman

A gigantic beauty of a stallion, fresh and responsive to my caresses.
Head high in the forehead, wide between the ears,
Limbs glossy and supple, tail dusting the ground,
Eyes full of sparkling wickedness, ears finely cut, flexibly moving.
His nostrils dilate as my heels embrace him,
His well-built limbs tremble with pleasure as we race around and return.

THE WRITER

Richard Wilbur

n her room at the prow of the house
Where light breaks, and the windows are tossed with linden,
My daughter is writing a story.

I pause in the stairwell, hearing
From her shut door a commotion of typewriter-keys
Like a chain hauled over a gunwale.

Young as she is, the stuff
Of her life is a great cargo, and some of it heavy:
I wish her a lucky passage.

But now it is she who pauses,
As if to reject my thought and its easy figure.
A stillness greatens, in which

The whole house seems to be thinking,
And then she is at it again with a bunched clamor
Of strokes, and again is silent.

I remember the dazed starling
Which was trapped in that very room, two years ago;
How we stole in, lifted a sash

And retreated, not to affright it;
And how for a helpless hour, through the crack of the door,
We watched the sleek, wild, dark

And iridescent creature
Batter against the brilliance, drop like a glove
To the hard floor, or the desk-top,

And wait then, humped and bloody,
For the wits to try it again; and how our spirits
Rose when, suddenly sure,

It lifted off from a chair-back,
Beating a smooth course for the right window
And clearing the sill of the world.

It is always a matter, my darling,
Of life or death, as I had forgotten. I wish
What I wished you before, but harder.

Jungle Tales
James Jebusa Shannon, 1895

WHEN MOTHER READS ALOUD

When Mother reads aloud, the past
 Seems real as every day;
I hear the tramp of armies vast,
I see the spears and lances cast,
 I join the trilling fray;
Brave knights and ladies fair and proud
I meet when Mother reads aloud.

When Mother reads aloud, far lands
 Seem very near and true;
I cross the desert's gleaming sands,
Or hunt the jungle's prowling bands,
 Or sail the ocean blue.
Far heights, whose peaks the cold mists shroud,
I scale, when Mother reads aloud.

When Mother reads aloud, I long
 For noble deeds to do—
To help the right, redress the wrong;
It seems so easy to be strong,
 So simple to be true.
Oh, thick and fast the visions crowd
My eyes, when Mother reads aloud.

11

Alexander Cassatt and His Son Robert
by Mary Cassatt, 1884–85

FATHER'S STORY

Elizabeth Madox Roberts

We put more coal on the big red fire,
And while we are waiting for dinner to cook,
Our father comes and tells us about
A story that he has read in a book.

And Charles and Will and Dick and I
And all of us but Clarence are there.
And some of us sit on Father's legs,
But one has to sit on the little red chair.

And when we are sitting very still,
He sings us a song or tells a piece;
He sings Dan Tucker Went to Town,
Or he tells us about the golden fleece.

He tells us about the golden wool,
And some of it is about a boy
Named Jason, and about a ship,
And some is about a town called Troy.

And while he is telling or singing it through,
I stand by his arm, for that is my place.
And I push my fingers into his skin
To make little dents in his big round face.

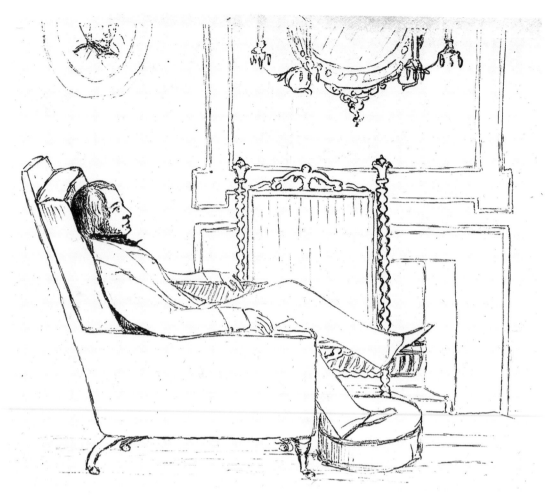

Henry Wadsworth Longfellow
1847

THE CHILDREN'S HOUR

Henry Wadsworth Longfellow

etween the dark and the daylight,
　　When the night is beginning to lower,
Comes a pause in the day's occupations
　　That is known as the Children's Hour.

I hear in the chamber above me
　　The patter of little feet,
The sound of a door that is opened,
　　And voices soft and sweet.

From my study I see in the lamplight,
　　Descending the broad hall stair,
Grave Alice, and laughing Allegra,
　　And Edith with golden hair.

A whisper, and then a silence:
　　Yet I know by their merry eyes
They are plotting and planning together
　　To take me by surprise.

A sudden rush from the stairway,
　　A sudden raid from the hall!
By three doors left unguarded
　　They enter my castle wall!

They climb up into my turret
　　O'er the arms and back of my chair;
If I try to escape, they surround me;
　　They seem to be everywhere.

The Daughters of Edward D. Boit
John Singer Sargent, 1882

They almost devour me with kisses,
   Their arms about me entwine,
Till I think of the Bishop of Bingen
   In his Mouse-Tower on the Rhine!

Do you think, O blue-eyed banditti,
   Because you have scaled the wall,
Such an old mustache as I am
   Is not a match for you all?

I have you fast in my fortress,
   And will not let you depart,
But put you down into the dungeon
   In the round-tower of my heart.

And there I will keep you forever,
   Yes, forever and a day,
Till the wall shall crumble to ruin,
   And molder in dust away!

The Old Woman Who Lived in a Shoe
about 1890

THERE WAS AN OLD WOMAN WHO LIVED IN A SHOE

There was an old woman who lived in a shoe,
She had so many children she didn't know what to do.
She gave them some broth, without any bread,
She whipped them all soundly and put them to bed.

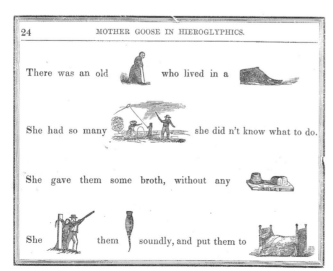

There Was An Old Woman Who Lived in a Shoe
about 1855

Little Johnny Green's First Experiment on Stilts
1879

TRY, TRY AGAIN

T. H. Palmer

is a lesson you should heed,
    Try, try again;
If at first you don't succeed,
    Try, try again;
Then your courage should appear,
For, if you will persevere,
You will conquer, never fear;
    Try, try again.

WOOD-CHUCK

How much wood would a wood-chuck chuck
If a wood-chuck could chuck wood?
He would chuck as much wood as a wood-chuck would chuck,
If a wood-chuck could chuck wood.

Woodchucks
John James Audubon, 1841

THE STAR

Jane Taylor

Twinkle, twinkle, little star,
How I wonder what you are!
Up above the world so high,
Like a diamond in the sky.

As your bright and tiny spark,
Lights the traveler in the dark—
Though I know not what you are,
Twinkle, twinkle, little star.

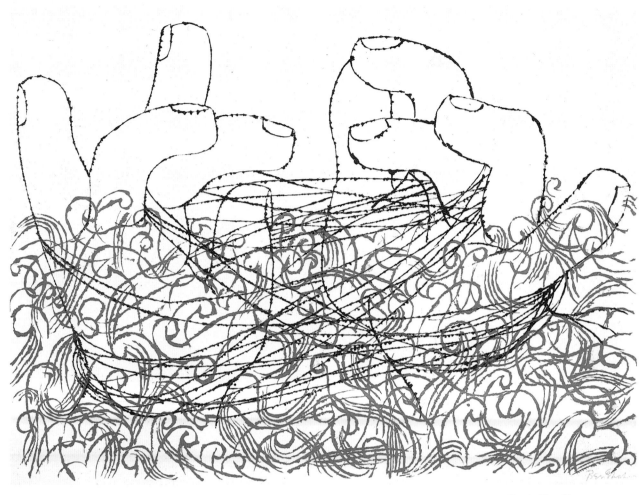

Cat's Cradle
Ben Shahn, 20th century

COUNTING-OUT RHYMES

enie, meenie, minie, mo,
Catch a tiger by the toe,
If he hollers let him go,
Eenie, meenie, minie, mo.

Out goes the rat,
Out goes the cat,
Out goes the lady
With the big green hat.
Y, O, U, spells you;
O, U, T, spells out!

One potato, two potato,
Three potato, four;
Five potato, six potato,
Seven potato, MORE.

One-ery, Ore-ery, Ickery, Ann,
Phillip-son, Phollop-son, Nicholas, John,
    Queevy, Quavy,
    English Navy,
Zinglum, Zanglum, Bolun, Bun.

Hinty, minty, cuty, corn,
Apple seed, and apple thorn,
Wire, briar, limber lock,
Three geese in a flock.
One flew east, and one flew west,
One flew over the cuckoo's nest.

19

The Far Side
by Gary Larson, 1980s

AFTER A VISIT TO THE NATURAL HISTORY MUSEUM

Laura E. Richards

This is the Wiggledywasticus,
   Very remarkable beast.
Nose to tail an eighth of a mile;
Took him an acre or two to smile;
Took him a quarter 'f an hour to wink;
Swallowed a pond for his morning drink.
Oh! would it had been vouchsafed to us
Upon the Wiggledywasticus
   Our wondering eyes to feast!

This is the Ptoodlecumtumpsydyl,
   Rather unusual bird.
Had a mouth before and behind;
Ate whichever way he 'd a mind;
Spoiled his digestion, so they say,
Pindled and dwindled quite away,
Or else he might have been living still,
The singular Ptoodlecumtumpsydyl.
   A pity, upon my word!

This is the Ichthyosnortoryx,
   Truly astonishing fish.
Used to snort in a terrible way;
Scared the lobsters to death, they say;
Had a nose like a tea-kettle spout;
Broke it snorting, and so died out.
Sad! if he had n't got into this fix,
We might have made of the 'Snortoryx
   A very acceptable dish.

60 Pigs for the N.Y.C. Sanitation Department
by Keith Haring, 1984

THIS LITTLE PIGGY
WENT TO MARKET

T his little piggy went to market,
This little piggy stayed home,
This little piggy had roast beef,
This little piggy had none,
And this little piggy cried "Wee, wee, wee,"
All the way home.

HOUSEBOAT MOUSE

Boathouse, Winter, Harlem River
Ernest Lawson, 1916

Charles Sullivan

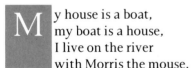y house is a boat,
my boat is a house,
I live on the river
with Morris the mouse.

He moved in with me
when the weather got cold
(I think he's a he—
but I'm not sure how old).

I found him one morning
asleep in my shoe,
and let him eat breakfast
with me—wouldn't you?

He has his own plate,
and a cup, but no spoon—
he likes dinner at eight,
half a bagel at noon.

When I go to work
he keeps watch on our things,
and when I get home
how he dances and sings!

He dances on tables,
he dances on deck,
he dances on ice
and a neighboring wreck.

He sings to the river,
the sky and the snow,
and sometimes I whisper
the words that I know.

And sometimes I whisper
the words that I know,
and sometimes just listen
to him and the snow.

Noah's Ark
Edward Hicks, 1848

OLD NOAH'S ARK

Old Noah once he built an ark,
And patched it up with hickory bark.
He anchored it to a great big rock,
And then he began to load his stock.
The animals went in one by one,
The elephant chewing a carroway bun.
The animals went in two by two,
The crocodile and the kangaroo.

The animals went in three by three,
The tall giraffe and the tiny flea,
The animals went in four by four,
The hippopotamus stuck in the door.
The animals went in five by five,
The bees mistook the bear for a hive.
The animals went in six by six,
The monkey was up to his usual tricks.
The animals went in seven by seven,
Said the ant to the elephant, "Who're ye shov'n?"
The animals went in eight by eight,
Some were early and some were late.
The animals went in nine by nine,
They all formed fours and marched in a line.
The animals went in ten by ten,
If you want any more, you can read it again. 23

Face Mask
Bella Coola (Indian Tribe)

MAGIC WORDS

(an Eskimo poem)

In the very earliest time,
when both people and animals lived on earth,
a person could become an animal if he wanted to
and an animal could become a human being.
Sometimes they were people
and sometimes animals
and there was no difference.
All spoke the same language.
That was the time when words were like magic.
The human mind had mysterious powers.
A word spoken by chance
might have strange consequences.
It would suddenly come alive
and what people wanted to happen could happen.
Nobody could explain this:
That's the way it was.

Blood Indian Tipis, Fort Macleod,
Alberta, Canada
Philip H. Godsell, 1949

WARRIOR NATION TRILOGY

(Cheyenne)

Lance Henson

1

from the mountains we come
lifting our voices for the beautiful
road you have given

we are the buffalo people
we dwell in the light of our father sun
in the shadow of our mother earth

we are the beautiful people
we roam the great plains without fear
in our days the land has taught us oneness
we alone breathe with the rivers
we alone hear the song of the stones

2

oh ghost that follows me
find in me strength to know the wisdom
of this life

take me to the mountain of my grandfather
i have heard him all night
singing among the summer leaves

3

great spirit

make me whole
i have come this day with my spirit
i am not afraid
for i have seen in vision
the white buffalo
grazing the frozen field
which grows near the full circle
of this
world

THE SHEAVES

Edwin Arlington Robinson

Where long the shadows of the wind had rolled,
Green wheat was yielding to the change assigned;
And as by some vast magic undivined
The world was turning slowly into gold.
Like nothing that was ever bought or sold
It waited there, the body and the mind;
And with a mighty meaning of a kind
That tells the more the more it is not told.

So in a land where all days are not fair,
Fair days went on till on another day
A thousand golden sheaves were lying there,
Shining and still, but not for long to stay—
As if a thousand girls with golden hair
Might rise from where they slept and go away.

Cradling Wheat
Thomas Hart Benton, 1938

Two Young American Indians from a Reservation in Southeastern Idaho
1897

A SONG OF GREATNESS

(a Chippewa Indian song)

Transcribed by Mary Austin

When I hear the old men
Telling of heroes,
Telling of great deeds
Of ancient days,
When I hear them telling,
Then I think within me
I too am one of these.

When I hear the people
Praising great ones,
Then I know that I too
Shall be esteemed,
I too when my time comes
Shall do mightily.

The Forty-Niners
Oscar E. Berninghaus, before 1942

WESTERN WAGONS

Rosemary and Stephen Vincent Benét

hey went with axe and rifle, when the trail was still to blaze
They went with wife and children, in the prairie-schooner days
With banjo and with frying pan—Susanna, don't you cry!
For I'm off to California to get rich out there or die!

We've broken land and cleared it, but we're tired of where we are.
They say that wild Nebraska is a better place by far.
There's gold in far Wyoming, there's black earth in Ioway,
So pack up the kids and blankets, for we're moving out today.

The cowards never started and the weak died on the road,
And all across the continent the endless campfires glowed
We'd taken land and settled—but a traveler passed by—
And we're going West tomorrow—Lordy, never ask us why!

We're going West tomorrow, where the promises can't fail.
O'er the hills in legions, boys, and crowd the dusty trail!
We shall starve and freeze and suffer. We shall die, and tame the lands.
But we're going West tomorrow, with our fortune in our hands.

A Mix Up
Charles M. Russell, 1910

WHOOPEE TI YI YO,
GIT ALONG, LITTLE DOGIES

As I walked out one morning for pleasure,
I spied a cowpuncher a-ridin' alone;
His hat was throwed back and his spurs was a-jinglin',
As he approached me a-singin' this song,

> *Whoopee ti yi yo, git along, little dogies,*
> *It's your misfortune, and none of my own.*
> *Whoopee ti yi yo, git along, little dogies,*
> *For you know Wyoming will be your new home.*

Early in the spring we round up the dogies,
Mark 'em and brand 'em and bob off their tails;
Round up our horses, load up the chuck-wagon,
Then throw the dogies upon the old trail.

It's whooping and yelling and driving the dogies;
Oh, how I wish you would go on!
It's whooping and punching and "Go on little dogies,
For you know Wyoming will be your new home."

Your mother she was raised way down in Texas,
Where the jimson weed and sandburs grow;
Now we'll fill you up on prickly pear and cholla
Till you are ready for the trail to Idaho.

Oh, you'll be soup for Uncle Sam's Injuns,—
It's "beef, heap beef," I hear them cry.
Git along, git along, git along, little dogies,
You're going to be beef steers by and by.

> *Whoopee ti yi yo, git along, little dogies,*
> *It's your misfortune, and none of my own.*
> *Whoopee ti yi yo, git along, little dogies,*
> *For you know Wyoming will be your new home.*

WHAT THE ENGINES SAID

(the joining of the Union Pacific and Central Pacific Railroads, May 10, 1869)

Bret Harte

What was it the Engines said,
Pilots touching,—head to head
Facing on the single track,
Half a world behind each back?
This is what the Engines said,
Unreported and unread.

With a prefatory screech,
In a florid Western speech,
Said the Engine from the WEST:
"I am from Sierra's crest;
And if altitude's a test,
Why, I reckon, it's confessed
That I've done my level best."

Said the Engine from the EAST:
"They who work best talk the least.
S'pose you whistle down your brakes;
What you've done is no great shakes,—
Pretty fair,—but let our meeting
Be a different kind of greeting.
Let these folks with champagne stuffing,
Not their Engines, do the *puffing*.

"Listen! Where Atlantic beats
Shores of snow and summer heats;
Where the Indian autumn skies
Paint the woods with wampum dyes,—
I have chased the flying sun,
Seeing all he looked upon,
Blessing all that he has blessed,
Nursing in my iron breast
All his vivifying heat,
All his clouds about my crest;
And before my flying feet
Every shadow must retreat."

Promontory, Utah, 1869

Said the Western Engine, "Phew!"
And a long, low whistle blew.
"Come, now, really that's the oddest
Talk for one so very modest.
You brag of your East! *You* do?
Why, *I* bring the East to *you!*
All the Orient, all Cathay,
Find through me the shortest way;
And the sun you follow here
Rises in my hemisphere.
Really,—if one must be rude,—
Length, my friend, ain't longitude."

Said the Union: "Don't reflect, or
I'll run over some Director."
Said the Central: "I'm Pacific;
But, when riled, I'm quite terrific.
Yet to-day we shall not quarrel,
Just to show these folks this moral,
How two Engines—in their vision—
Once have met without collision."

This is what the Engines said,
Unreported and unread;
Spoken slightly through the nose,
With a whistle at the close.

SCHOOLCRAFT'S DIARY
WRITTEN ON THE MISSOURI:
1830

Robert Bly

Waters are loose: from Judith and the Larb,
Straining and full, the thick Missouri, choked
With sticks and roots, and high with floating trees,
And spoils of snowfields from the Crazy Hills,
Burns loose earth off. The brown Missouri's mouth
Eats earth a hundred feet below the plains.
At dawn we see the crumbling cliffs at first,
Then horse and rider, then the eastern sky.
At daybreak riders shout from western cliffs.
The buffalo, in herds, come down to drink,
Turn back, and shoulders humping, racket on
Up dust-chewn paths onto the plains of dust;
And I have heard the buffalo stampede
With muffled clatter of colliding horns.
A subtle peril hangs above this land
Like smoke that floats at dawn above dead fires.

The dead in scaffolds float on steady rafts,
Corroding in their sepulchers of air.
At dawn the Osage part their tepee doors,
Cutting their arms and thighs with sharp-edged shells.
The dark-blue buzzard flocks awake on trees
And stretch their black wings toward the sun to dry.
Such are the few details that I have seen.

And there are signs of what will come: the whites
With steep traps hanging, swung from saddle thongs.
The busy whites believe these Sioux and Kaws
And Mandans are not men at all, but beasts:
Some snake-bound beast, regressed, embedded, wound,
Held in damnation, and by death alone
To be released. The Sioux are still and silent
Generally, and I have watched them stand
By ones and twos upon the riverbank,
As still as Hudson's blankets winding them,
While shuttling steamboats, smoking, labor up,
Invading the landscape of their youth and dreams,
Pushed up, they say, by smoke; and they believe
This tribe of whites, like smoke, soon shall return
From where it came. The truth drops out of mind,
As if the pain of action were so great
And life so freezing and Medusa-faced
That, like Medusa's head, it could be held
And not observed, lest its reward be stone.

Fur Traders Descending the Missouri
by George Caleb Bingham, 1845

Now night grows old above this riverboat.
Before I end, I shall include account
Of incident tonight that moved my wonder.
At dusk we tied the ship to trees on shore;
No mortal boat in these night shoals can live.
At first I heard a cry: then shufflings, steps.
The muffled sounds on deckoak overhead
Drew me on deck. The air was chill, and there
I sensed, because these senses here are sharp
And must be, something living and unknown.
To night and north a crowd stared from the boatrail,
Upriver, northward, nightward; a speck of white.
The thing was white: the resonance of night
Returned its whiffs and whistlings on the air.
The frontier men swore in that river thicket,
In ambush like the lizards they're modeled on,
Bristling for war, would be a thresh of Sioux.
And gamblers, nudging the settlers, baiting them:
"Along the river there's some settler's cow!
Maybe a pagan pig, some Poland China,
The settler could not keep inside his crib.
He's free, and terrorizing catfish now."
But Mormons see some robe in that faint white,
An angel of death upon the chill Missouri.

One man believed that there was nothing there,
As the moon is false, and all its light is false.
I felt a fear, as if it were protected.
When the talk died, eight men, and I with them,
Set off and, moving overboard in dark,
With guns, protected by the thunder's noise,
Up the dark stream, toward where the splashes rose,
So armed in case of Sioux, to our surprise
We found a white and wounded Northern Bear,
Shot in that day about the snout and head.
The pure-white bear, not native to these parts,
But to the Horns, or Ranges, born, and shot
That morning, had turned west or south in pain,
And had apparently through these dry plains
Turned west, to lay its burning paws and head
And place its fever-proud and festered flesh
Within the cool Missouri's turbid bed.
I felt as I had once when through a door,
At ten or twelve, I'd seen my mother bathing.
Soon after, clouds of rain drove us indoors,
And lightning; swift rain fell in sheets; such rain
Said to be sudden in these Western lands.
Minutes before it broke, a circling mass
Of split-tail swallows came and then were gone.

WHERE
MOUNTAIN LION
LAY DOWN
WITH DEER

(Laguna Pueblo, February 1973)

Leslie Marmon Silko

I climb the black rock mountain
    stepping from day to day
                silently.
I smell the wind for my ancestors
    pale blue leaves
    crushed wild mountain smell.
Returning
  up the gray stone cliff
  where I descended
              a thousand years ago.
Returning to faded black stone
  where mountain lion lay down with deer.
It is better to stay up here
              watching wind's reflection
              in tall yellow flowers.
The old ones who remember me are gone
     the old songs are all forgotten
and the story of my birth.
How I danced in snow-frost moonlight
     distant stars to the end of the Earth,
How I swam away
           in freezing mountain water
           narrow mossy canyon tumbling down
                out of the mountain
                out of deep canyon stone
          down
             the memory
                spilling out
                into the world.

Ancient Ruins in the Canyon de Chelly, Arizona
Timothy H. O'Sullivan, 1873

THE PLACE WHERE A GREAT CITY STANDS

from *Song of the Broad-Axe*

Walt Whitman

The place where a great city stands is not the place of stretch'd wharves, docks,
        manufactures, deposits of produce merely,
Nor the place of ceaseless salutes of new-comers or the anchor-lifters of the
        departing,
Nor the place of the tallest and costliest buildings or shops selling goods from
        the rest of the earth,
Nor the place of the best libraries and schools, nor the place where money is
        plentiest,
Nor the place of the most numerous population.

Where the city stands with the brawniest breed of orators and bards,
Where the city stands that is belov'd by these, and loves them in return and
        understands them,
Where no monuments exist to heroes but in the common words and deeds,
Where thrift is in its place, and prudence is in its place,
Where the men and women think lightly of the laws,
Where the slave ceases and the master of slaves ceases,
Where the populace rise at once against the never-ending audacity of elected
        persons,
Where fierce men and women pour forth as the sea to the whistle of death pours
        its sweeping and unript waves,
Where outside authority enters always after the precedence of inside authority,

Where the citizen is always the head and ideal, and President, Mayor,
        Governor and what not, are agents for pay,
Where children are taught to be laws to themselves, and to depend on
        themselves,
Where equanimity is illustrated in affairs,
Where speculations on the soul are encouraged,
Where women walk in public processions in the streets the same as the men,
Where they enter the public assembly and take places the same as the men;
Where the city of the faithfulest friends stands,
Where the city of the cleanliness of the sexes stands,
Where the city of the healthiest fathers stands,
Where the city of the best-bodied mothers stands,
There the great city stands.

39

SKYSCRAPER Carl Sandburg

By day the skyscraper looms in the smoke and sun and has a soul.
Prairie and valley, streets of the city, pour people into it and they mingle among its twenty floors and are poured out again back to the streets, prairies and valleys.
It is the men and women, boys and girls so poured in and out all day that give the building a soul of dreams and thoughts and memories.
(Dumped in the sea or fixed in a desert, who would care for the building or speak its name or ask a policeman the way to it?)

Elevators slide on their cables and tubes catch letters and parcels and iron pipes carry gas and water in and sewage out.
Wires climb with secrets, carry light and carry words, and tell terrors and profits and loves—curses of men grappling plans of business and questions of women in plots of love.

Hour by hour the caissons reach down to the rock of the earth and hold the building to a turning planet.
Hour by hour the girders play as ribs and reach out and hold together the stone walls and floors.
Hour by hour the hand of the mason and the stuff of the mortar clinch the pieces and parts to the shape an architect voted.
Hour by hour the sun and the rain, the air and the rust, and the press of time running into centuries, play on the building inside and out and use it.

Men who sunk the pilings and mixed the mortar are laid in graves where the wind whistles a wild song without words
And so are men who strung the wires and fixed the pipes and tubes and those who saw it rise floor by floor.
Souls of them all are here, even the hod carrier begging at back doors hundreds of miles away and the bricklayer who went to state's prison for shooting another man while drunk.
(One man fell from a girder and broke his neck at the end of a straight plunge—he is here—his soul has gone into the stones of the building.)

On the office doors from tier to tier—hundreds of names and each name standing for a face written across with a dead child, a passionate lover, a driving ambition for a million dollar business or a lobster's ease of life.

Behind the signs on the doors they work and the walls tell nothing from room to room.
Ten-dollar-a-week stenographers take letters from corporation officers, lawyers, efficiency engineers, and tons of letters go bundled from the building to all ends of the earth.
Smiles and tears of each office girl go into the soul of the building just the same as the master-men who rule the building.

*New York City: Showing the Construction of the Esso Building
as Iron Workers Raise Steel at the 32nd Floor*
1954

Hands of clocks turn to noon hours and each floor empties its men and
    women who go away and eat and come back to work.
Toward the end of the afternoon all work slackens and all jobs go
    slower as the people feel day closing on them.
One by one the floors are emptied. . . . The uniformed elevator men are
    gone. Pails clang. . . . Scrubbers work, talking in foreign
    tongues. Broom and water and mop clean from the floors human
    dust and spit, and machine grime of the day.
Spelled in electric fire on the roof are words telling miles of houses and
    people where to buy a thing for money. The sign speaks till
    midnight.

Darkness on the hallways. Voices echo. Silence holds. . . . Watchmen
    walk slow from floor to floor and try the doors. Revolvers bulge
    from their hip pockets. . . . Steel safes stand in corners. Money is
    stacked in them.
A young watchman leans at a window and sees the lights of barges but-
    ting their way across a harbor, nets of red and white lanterns
    in a railroad yard, and a span of glooms splashed with lines of
    white and blurs of crosses and clusters over the sleeping city.
By night the skyscraper looms in the smoke and the stars and has
    a soul.

New York, Uptown, Downtown
Franco Zavani, 1988

THEATRE HOUR

Ogden Nash

he hotel doorman's frantic whistle
Makes rugged taxi drivers bristle.
The doormen chittering like grackles
Only raise the hacky's hackles.
Contemptuously stares the cabby
Like a bobcat at a tabby,
Then with derisive farewell honks
Heads happily homeward to the Bronx.
That's why, my children, I'm afraidy
That you'll be late for "My Fair Lady."

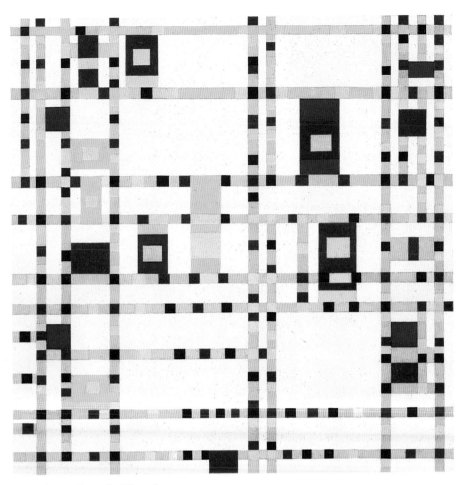

Broadway Boogie Woogie
Piet Mondrian, 1942–43

IT IS NO DREAM OF MINE

Henry David Thoreau

It is no dream of mine,
To ornament a line;
I cannot come nearer to God and Heaven
Than I live to Walden even.
I am its stony shore,
And the breeze that passes o'er;
In the hollow of my hand
Are its water and its sand,
And its deepest resort
Lies high in my thought.

ANALYSIS OF BASEBALL

May Swenson

It's about
the ball,
the bat,
and the mitt.
Ball hits
bat, or it
hits mitt.
Bat doesn't
hit ball, bat
meets it.
Ball bounces
off bat, flies
air, or thuds
ground (dud)
or it
fits mitt.

Bat waits
for ball
to mate.
Ball hates
to take bat's
bait. Ball
flirts, bat's
late, don't
keep the date.
Ball goes in
(thwack) to mitt,
and goes out
(thwack) back
to mitt.

Hank Aaron Hits Home Run Number 715

Ball fits
mitt, but
not all
the time.
Sometimes
ball gets hit
(pow) when bat
meets it,
and sails
to a place
where mitt
has to quit
in disgrace.
That's about
the bases
loaded,
about 40,000
fans exploded.

It's about
the ball,
the bat,
the mitt,
the bases
and the fans.
It's done
on a diamond,
and for fun.
It's about
home, and it's
about run.

ROCK 'N' ROLL BAND

Shel Silverstein

If we were a rock 'n' roll band,
We'd travel all over the land.
We'd play and we'd sing and wear spangly things,
If we were a rock 'n' roll band.

If we were a rock 'n' roll band,
And we were up there on the stand,
The people would hear us and love us and cheer us,
Hurray for that rock 'n' roll band.

Talking Heads on Tour
Clayton Call, 1982

If we were a rock 'n' roll band,
Then we'd have a million fans.
We'd giggle and laugh and sign autographs,
If we were a rock 'n' roll band.

If we were a rock 'n' roll band,
The people would all kiss our hands.
We'd be millionaires and have extra long hair,
If we were a rock 'n' roll band.

But we ain't no rock 'n' roll band,
We're just seven kids in the sand
With homemade guitars and pails and jars
And drums of potato chip cans.

Just seven kids in the sand,
Talkin' and wavin' our hands,
And dreamin' and thinkin' oh wouldn't it be grand,
If we were a rock 'n' roll band.

THE SONG OF THE JELLICLES

T. S. Eliot

Jellicle Cats come out tonight,
Jellicle Cats come one come all:
The Jellicle Moon is shining bright—
Jellicles come to the Jellicle Ball.

Jellicle Cats are black and white,
Jellicle Cats are rather small;
Jellicle Cats are merry and bright,
And pleasant to hear when they caterwaul.
Jellicle Cats have cheerful faces,
Jellicle Cats have bright black eyes;
They like to practice their airs and graces
And wait for the Jellicle Moon to rise.

Jellicle Cats develop slowly,
Jellicle Cats are not too big;
Jellicle Cats are roly-poly,
They know how to dance a gavotte and a jig.
Until the Jellicle Moon appears
They make their toilette and take their repose:
Jellicles wash behind their ears,
Jellicles dry between their toes.

Jellicle Cats are white and black,
Jellicle Cats are of moderate size;
Jellicles jump like a jumping-jack,
Jellicle Cats have moonlit eyes.
They're quiet enough in the morning hours,
They're quiet enough in the afternoon,
Reserving their terpsichorean powers
To dance by the light of the Jellicle Moon.

Jellicle Cats are black and white,
Jellicle Cats (as I said) are small;
If it happens to be a stormy night
They will practice a caper or two in the hall.
If it happens the sun is shining bright
You would say they had nothing to do at all:
They are resting and saving themselves to be right
For the Jellicle Moon and the Jellicle Ball.

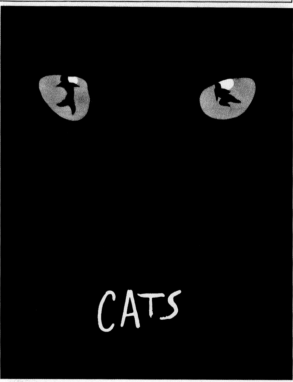

Playbill® Cover
for the Broadway Musical "Cats™"
October 7, 1982

Laughing Cat
Roy Lichtenstein, 1961

Bronx, New York, (Elephant's Trunk)
by Garry Winogrand, 1960s

THE ELEPHANT'S TRUNK

Alice Wilkins

The elephant always carries his trunk,
I couldn't do that with my own.
His trunk is a part of himself, you see—
It's part of his head—it's grown!

ELETELEPHONY

Laura E. Richards

Once there was an elephant,
Who tried to use the telephant—
No! no! I mean an elephone
Who tried to use the telephone—
(Dear me! I am not certain quite
That even now I've got it right.)

Howe'er it was, he got his trunk
Entangled in the telephunk;
The more he tried to get it free,
The louder buzzed the telephee—
(I fear I 'd better drop the song
Of elephop and telephong!)

THE TELEPHONE

Robert Frost

"When I was just as far as I could walk
From here today,
There was an hour
All still
When leaning with my head against a flower
I heard you talk.
Don't say I didn't, for I heard you say—
You spoke from that flower on the windowsill—
Do you remember what it was you said?"

"First tell me what it was you thought you heard."

"Having found the flower and driven a bee away,
I leaned my head,
And holding by the stalk,
I listened and I thought I caught the word—
What was it? Did you call me by my name?
Or did you say—
Someone said 'Come'—I heard it as I bowed."

"I may have thought as much, but not aloud."

"Well, so I came."

(Untitled)
by Keith Haring, 1987

DIGGING FOR CHINA

Richard Wilbur

"Far enough down is China," somebody said.
"Dig deep enough and you might see the sky
As clear as at the bottom of a well.
Except it would be real—a different sky.
Then you could burrow down until you came
To China! Oh, it's nothing like New Jersey.
There's people, trees, and houses, and all that,
But much, much different. Nothing looks the same."

I went and got the trowel out of the shed
And sweated like a coolie all that morning,
Digging a hole beside the lilac-bush,
Down on my hands and knees. It was a sort
Of praying, I suspect. I watched my hand
Dig deep and darker, and I tried and tried
To dream a place where nothing was the same.
The trowel never did break through to blue.

Before the dream could weary of itself
My eyes were tired of looking into darkness,
My sunbaked head of hanging down a hole.
I stood up in a place I had forgotten,
Blinking and staggering while the earth went round
And showed me silver barns, the fields dozing
In palls of brightness, patens growing and gone
In the tides of leaves, and the whole sky china blue.
Until I got my balance back again
All that I saw was China, China, China.

READING IN THE AUTUMN

Shen Chou

(translation of poem that appears in the painting)

he big trees exposed to the west wind are losing their leaves.
To be comfortable I have unfastened the collar of my robe;
   sitting here, I'm letting the time go by.
Doing nothing, I've turned my back on encroaching autumn. . . .
   I've not finished my book.
My spirit has gone wandering in the sky. . . . Who can fathom it?

Reading in the Autumn
Shen Chou, about 1470

HIGH FLIGHT

John Gillespie Magee, Jr.

O h, I have slipped the surly bonds of earth,
And danced the skies on laughter-silvered wings;
Sunward I've climbed and joined the tumbling mirth
Of sun-split clouds—and done a hundred things
You have not dreamed of—wheeled and soared and swung
High in the sunlit silence. Hov'ring there
I've chased the shouting wind along and flung
My eager craft through footless halls of air.
Up, up the long delirious burning blue
I've topped the wind-swept heights with easy grace,
Where never lark, or even eagle, flew;
And, while with silent, lifting mind I've trod
The high untrespassed sanctity of space,
Put out my hand, and touched the face of God.

Astronaut Edward H. White (Gemini IV),
the First American to "Float in Space"
June 3, 1965

Africa and Other Areas of the Earth, Seen from Apollo 17 Spacecraft

METAPHOR FOR MY SON

John Holmes

hope when you're yourself and twice my age
Still you'll rake your heart in unreasonable rage
At the imperfect praise of perfect things,
If in all the weathers of your mind and power
You work to stretch the best of fliers' wings.
I've seen the landsmen tire their legs in an hour.

And I hope you'll have a son a flier who fights
Your old-fashioned praise of earlier heights.
But may his son remember the three of us,
And understand our impatient angry pride.
Let the wind blow in our lifetime long to bless
Good wings, and you be one to see them ride

As I see them soar up the bright streams of air,
Hang, wing away, shine in the shine of bare
Sunlight pouring toward earth in middle day.
You'll see man's power alive in grace; then see
The grounded watchers stare up and turn away.
I say, Curse them. And may you always be

Angry as I am when the tough, the rare, the tall
Fliers with all their wisdom burn and fall.
I hope you'll live to learn to rage at their death
Too young by unnatural causes away from the field.
I want you to measure as I have measured breath
Then, and to keep the deep wells of grief sealed.

This will be hard on you, but high is hard.
I want you to tell our sons I cursed; I cared.
And forget me. Tell them it was not always so
That all men clambered on any climbing thing
To drag it down. You'll tell them, once you know,
Even once, air running over and under the wing,

Wind trying and shaping the immeasurable air
To a map of the coasts of heaven forever clear.
Fear will be tied around your wrist. But fliers
Before our time have had that weight there, too,
And heard the long wind screaming through the wires,
And have done what they have told themselves to do.

Man and Fighter: U. S. Air Force Col. Daniel "Chappie" James, Jr.,
in Front of His F-4C Phantom in Southeast Asia

The Turbulent Sixties
Roger Brown, 1983

SOUTHBOUND ON THE FREEWAY

May Swenson

tourist came in from Orbitville,
parked in the air, and said:

The creatures of this star
are made of metal and glass.

Through the transparent parts
you can see their guts.

Their feet are round and roll
on diagrams or long

measuring tapes, dark
with white lines.

They have four eyes.
The two in back are red.

Sometimes you can see a five-eyed
one, with a red eye turning

on the top of his head.
He must be special —

the others respect him
and go slow

when he passes, winding
among them from behind.

They all hiss as they glide,
like inches, down the marked

tapes. Those soft shapes,
shadowy inside

the hard bodies — are they
their guts or their brains?

BOY READING

John Holmes

ot yet. Not yet," between the lines
I read in urgent shifting signs.
I could not, must not, go to bed
Until I knew what the whole book said.
"Here is a hundred-year-old day
In words forever wearing away,
Tall with ships, and loud with men,
And over the page the guns again,
And over the page again the words
Locked in onward flight like birds."
Troy was falling, in blood and dust.
Confederate swords were dark with rust.
An English ship at noon went down.
A big shell burst in a country town.
I was a child who turned the page
With a reader's right and hungry rage
To take the meaning and make it his.
There in the book it was, and is,
For always, reading, I looked away
At things the book could never say.
The green lamp shone in evening air.
All that I knew of good was there.
Bedtime came, and the end of the book,
But out to the dark of sleep I took
The dreams that fade, but never cease,
The words of war in the house of peace.

PAUL REVERE'S RIDE

Henry Wadsworth Longfellow

Listen, my children, and you shall hear
Of the midnight ride of Paul Revere,
On the eighteenth of April, in Seventy-five;
Hardly a man is now alive
Who remembers that famous day and year.

He said to his friend, "If the British march
By land or sea from the town tonight,
Hang a lantern aloft in the belfry arch
Of the North Church tower as a signal light,—
One, if by land, and two, if by sea;
And I on the opposite shore will be,
Ready to ride and spread the alarm
Through every Middlesex village and farm,
For the country folk to be up and to arm."

Then he said, "Good night!" and with muffled oar
Silently rowed to the Charlestown shore,
Just as the moon rose over the bay,
Where swinging wide at her moorings lay
The Somerset, British man-of-war;
A phantom ship, with each mast and spar
Across the moon like a prison bar,
And a huge black hulk, that was magnified
By its own reflection in the tide.

Meanwhile, his friend, through alley and street,
Wanders and watches with eager ears,
Till in the silence around him he hears
The muster of men at the barrack door,
The sound of arms, and the tramp of feet,
And the measured tread of the grenadiers,
Marching down to their boats on the shore.

Then he climbed the tower of the Old North Church,
By the wooden stairs, with stealthy tread,
To the belfry-chamber overhead,
And startled the pigeons from their perch
On the somber rafters, that round him made
Masses and moving shapes of shade,—
By the trembling ladder, steep and tall,
To the highest window in the wall,
Where he paused to listen and look down
A moment on the roofs of the town,
And the moonlight flowing over all.

Beneath, in the churchyard, lay the dead,
In their night-encampment on the hill,
Wrapped in silence so deep and still
That he could hear, like a sentinel's tread,
The watchful night-wind, as it went
Creeping along from tent to tent,
And seeming to whisper, "All is well!"
A moment only he feels the spell
Of the place and the hour, and the secret dread
Of the lonely belfry and the dead;
For suddenly all his thoughts are bent
On a shadowy something far away,
Where the river widens to meet the bay,—
A line of black that blends and floats
On the rising tide, like a bridge of boats.

Meanwhile, impatient to mount and ride,
Booted and spurred, with a heavy stride
On the opposite shore walked Paul Revere.
Now he patted his horse's side,
Now gazed at the landscape far and near,
Then, impetuous, stamped the earth,
And turned and tightened his saddle-girth;
But mostly he watched with eager search
The belfry-tower of the Old North Church,
As it rose above the graves on the hill,
Lonely and spectral and somber and still.
And lo! as he looks, on the belfry's height
A glimmer, and then a gleam of light!
He springs to the saddle, the bridle he turns,
But lingers and gazes, till full on his sight
A second lamp in the belfry burns!

A hurry of hoofs in a village street,
A shape in the moonlight, a bulk in the dark,
And beneath, from the pebbles, in passing, a spark
Struck out by a steed flying fearless and fleet;
That was all! And yet, through the gloom and the light
The fate of a nation was riding that night;
And the spark struck out by that steed in his flight,
Kindled the land into flame with its heat.

He has left the village and mounted the steep,
And beneath him, tranquil and broad and deep,
Is the Mystic, meeting the ocean tides;
And under the alders, that skirt its edge,
Now soft on the sand, now loud on the ledge,
Is heard the tramp of his steed as he rides.

It was twelve by the village clock
When he crossed the bridge into Medford town.
He heard the crowing of the cock,
And the barking of the farmer's dog,
And felt the damp of the river fog,
That rises after the sun goes down.

It was one by the village clock,
When he galloped into Lexington.
He saw the gilded weathercock
Swim in the moonlight as he passed,
And the meeting-house windows, blank and bare,
Gaze at him with a spectral glare,
As if they already stood aghast
At the bloody work they would look upon.

It was two by the village clock,
When he came to the bridge in Concord town.
He heard the bleating of the flock,
And the twitter of birds among the trees,
And felt the breath of the morning breeze
Blowing over the meadows brown.
And one was safe and asleep in his bed
Who at the bridge would be first to fall,
Who that day would be lying dead,
Pierced by a British musket-ball.

You know the rest. In the books you have read,
How the British Regulars fired and fled,—
How the farmers gave them ball for ball,
From behind each fence and farmyard wall,
Chasing the redcoats down the lane,
Then crossing the fields to emerge again
Under the trees at the turn of the road,
And only pausing to fire and load.

So through the night rode Paul Revere;
And so through the night went his cry of alarm
To every Middlesex village and farm,—
A cry of defiance, and not of fear,
A voice in the darkness, a knock at the door,
And a word that shall echo forevermore!
For, borne on the night-wind of the Past,
Through all our history, to the last,
In the hour of darkness and peril and need,
The people will waken and listen to hear
The hurrying hoofbeats of that steed,
And the midnight message of Paul Revere.

Paul Revere
John Singleton Copley, 1768–1770

ON FREEDOM

James Russell Lowell

They are slaves who fear to speak
For the fallen and the weak;
They are slaves who will not choose
Hatred, scoffing, and abuse,
Rather than in silence shrink
From the truth they needs must think;
They are slaves who dare not be
In the right with two or three.

Phillis Wheatley
artist unknown, 1773

SHOULD YOU, MY LORD

From *To The Right Honorable William, Earl of Dartmouth,*
His Majesty's Principal Secretary of State for North America, etc.

Phillis Wheatley

Should you, my lord, while you pursue my song
Wonder from whence my love of *Freedom* sprung,
Whence flow these wishes for the common good,
By feeling hearts alone best understood,
I, young in life, by seeming cruel fate
Was snatch'd from *Afric's* fancy'd happy seat:
What pangs excruciating must molest,
What sorrows labour in my parent's breast?
Steel'd was the soul and by no misery mov'd
That from a father seiz'd his babe belov'd
Such, such my case. And can I then but pray
Others may never feel tyrannic sway?

CAPTAIN MOLLY

William Collins

On the bloody field of Monmouth
    Flashed the guns of Greene and Wayne,
Fiercely roared the tide of battle,
    Thick the sward was heaped with slain.
Foremost, facing death and danger,
    Hessian, horse, and grenadier,
In the vanguard, fiercely fighting,
    Stood an Irish Cannonier.

Loudly roared his iron cannon,
    Mingling ever in the strife,
And beside him, firm and daring,
    Stood his faithful Irish wife.
Of her bold contempt of danger
    Greene and Lee's Brigades could tell,
Every one knew "Captain Molly,"
    And the army loved her well.

Surged the roar of battle round them,
    Swiftly flew the iron hail,
Forward dashed a thousand bayonets,
    That lone battery to assail.
From the foeman's foremost columns
    Swept a furious fusillade,
Mowing down the massed battalions
    In the ranks of Greene's Brigade.

Fast and faster worked the gunner,
    Soiled with powder, blood, and dust,
English bayonets shone before him,
    Shot and shell around him burst;
Still he fought with reckless daring,
    Stood and manned her long and well,
Till at last the gallant fellow
    Dead—beside his cannon fell.

With a bitter cry of sorrow,
    And a dark and angry frown,
Looked that band of gallant patriots,
    At their gunner stricken down.
"Fall back, comrades, it is folly
    Thus to strive against the foe."
"No! not so," cried Irish Molly;
    "We can strike another blow."

Quickly leaped she to the cannon,
    In her fallen husband's place,
Sponged and rammed it fast and steady,
    Fired it in the foeman's face.
Flashed another ringing volley,
    Roared another from the gun;
"Boys, hurrah!" cried gallant Molly,
    "For the flag of Washington."

Greene's Brigade, though shorn and shattered,
    Slain and bleeding half their men,
When they heard that Irish slogan,
    Turned and charged the foe again.
Knox and Wayne and Morgan rally,
    To the front they forward wheel,
And before their rushing onset
    Clinton's English columns reel.

Still the cannon's voice in anger
    Rolled and rattled o'er the plain,
Till there lay in swarms around it
    Mangled heaps of Hessian slain.
"Forward! charge them with the bayonet!"
    'Twas the voice of Washington,
And there burst a fiery greeting
    From the Irish woman's gun.

Monckton falls; against his columns
    Leap the troops of Wayne and Lee,
And before their reeking bayonets
    Clinton's red battalions flee.
Morgan's rifles, fiercely flashing,
    Thin the foe's retreating ranks,
And behind them onward dashing
    Ogden hovers on their flanks.

Fast they fly, these boasting Britons,
    Who in all their glory came,
With their brutal Hessian hirelings
    To wipe out our country's name.
Proudly floats the starry banner,
    Monmouth's glorious field is won,
And in triumph Irish Molly
    Stands beside her smoking gun.

George Washington
Gilbert Stuart, 1796

WASHINGTON MONUMENT BY NIGHT

Carl Sandburg

1

he stone goes straight.
A lean swimmer dives into night sky,
Into half-moon mist.

2

Two trees are coal black.
This is a great white ghost between.
It is cool to look at.
Strong men, strong women, come here.

3

Eight years is a long time
To be fighting all the time.

4

The republic is a dream.
Nothing happens unless first a dream.

*Workmen Completing
the Washington Monument,* 1884

5

The wind bit hard at Valley Forge one Christmas.
Soldiers tied rags on their feet.
Red footprints wrote on the snow . . .
. . . and stone shoots into stars here
. . . into half-moon mist tonight.

6

Tongues wrangled dark at a man.
He buttoned his overcoat and stood alone.
In a snowstorm, red hollyberries, thoughts, he stood alone.

7

Women said: He is lonely
. . . fighting . . . fighting . . . eight years . . .

8

The name of an iron man goes over the world.
It takes a long time to forget an iron man.

WOULD YOU HEAR OF AN OLD-TIME SEA FIGHT?

(about John Paul Jones, September 23, 1779)

Walt Whitman

Would you hear of an old-time sea fight?
Would you hear who won by the light of the moon and stars?
List to the yarn as my grandmother's father the sailor told it to me.

Our foe was no sulk in his ship I tell you (said he,)
His was the surly English pluck, and there is no tougher or
                truer, and never was, and never will be;
Along the lower'd eve he came horribly raking at us.
We closed with him, the yards entangled, the cannon touched.
My captain lashed fast with his own hands.

We had received some eighteen pound shots under the water,
On the lower gun deck two large pieces had burst at the
    first fire, killing all around and blowing up overhead.

Fighting at sundown, fighting at dark,
Ten o'clock at night, the full moon well up, our leaks on
                the gain, the five feet of water reported,
The master-at-arms loosing the prisoners confined in the
                after hold to give them a chance for themselves.

The transit to and from the magazine is now stopped by the sentinels,
They see so many strange faces they do not know whom to trust.
Our frigate takes fire,
The other asks if we demand quarter?
If our colors are struck and the fighting done?

John Paul Jones,
Jean-Antoine Houdon, 1780

Battle Between John Paul Jones's Bonhomme Richard *and Richard Pearson's* Serapis
B. F. Leizalt, about 1781

Now I laugh content, for I hear the voice of my little captain,
We have not struck, he composedly cries, *we have just*
        begun our part of the fighting.

Only three guns are in use,
One is directed by the captain himself against the enemy's mainmast,
Two well-serv'd with grape and canister silence his musketry and clear his decks.

The tops alone second the fire of this little battery, especially the maintop,
They hold out bravely during the whole of the action.
Not a moment's cease,
The leaks gain fast on the pumps, the fire eats toward the powder magazine.

One of the pumps has been shot away, it is generally thought we are sinking.

Serene stands the little captain,
He is not hurried, his voice is neither high nor low,
His eyes give more light to us than our battle lanterns.

Toward twelve there in the beams of the moon they surrender to us.

Walt Whitman with Nigel and Catherine Jeanette Cholmeley-Jones
George Collins Cox, about 1887

I AM OF OLD AND YOUNG

from *Song of Myself*

Walt Whitman

 am of old and young, of the foolish as much as the wise,
Regardless of others, ever regardful of others,
Maternal as well as paternal, a child as well as a man,
Stuff'd with the stuff that is coarse and stuff'd with the stuff
    that is fine,
One of the Nation of many nations, the smallest the same
    and the largest the same,
A Southerner soon as a Northerner, a planter nonchalant
    and hospitable down by the Oconee I live,
A Yankee bound my own way ready for trade, my joints the
    limberest joints on earth and the sternest joints on earth,
A Kentuckian walking the vale of the Elkhorn in my deerskin
    leggings, a Louisianian or Georgian,
A boatman over lakes or bays or along coasts, a Hoosier, Badger,
    Buckeye;
At home on Kanadian snow-shoes or up in the bush, or with
    fishermen off Newfoundland,
At home in the fleet of ice-boats, sailing with the rest and tacking,
At home on the hills of Vermont or in the woods of Maine, or
    the Texan ranch,
Comrade of Californians, comrade of free North-Westerners,
    (loving their big proportions,)
Comrade of raftsmen and coalmen, comrade of all who shake
    hands and welcome to drink and meat,
A learner with the simplest, a teacher of the thoughtfullest,
A novice beginning yet experient of myriads of seasons,
Of every hue and caste am I, of every rank and religion,
A farmer, mechanic, artist, gentleman, sailor, quaker,
Prisoner, fancy-man, rowdy, lawyer, physician, priest.

I resist any thing better than my own diversity,
Breathe the air but leave plenty after me,
And am not stuck up, and am in my place.

Abraham Lincoln reading with his son Tad
Mathew B. Brady, 1860s

Chest Showing Spanish Dancers and Cowboy
about 1820

THERE WAS A ROOF
OVER OUR HEADS

from *Lost on September Trail, 1967*

Alberto Ríos

here was a roof over our heads
and that was at least something.
Then came dances.
The energy for them came from
childhood, or before, from the time
when only warmth was important.
We had come to the New World
and become part of it.
If the roof would shelter us,
we would keep it in repair.
Roof then could be roof,
solid, visible, recognizable,
and we could be whatever it was
that we were at this moment.
Having lost our previous names
somewhere in the rocks as we ran,
we could not yet describe ourselves.

Over the River to Grandmother's House
Grandma Moses, 1945

THANKSGIVING DAY

Lydia Maria Child

ver the river and through the wood,
    To grandfather's house we go;
      The horse knows the way
      To carry the sleigh
    Through the white and drifted snow.

Over the river and through the wood—
    Oh, how the wind does blow!
      It stings the toes
      And bites the nose,
    As over the ground we go.

Over the river and through the wood,
    To have a first-rate play.
      Hear the bells ring,
      "Ting-a-ling-ding!"
    Hurrah for Thanksgiving Day!

Over the river and through the wood
    Trot fast, my dapple-gray!
      Spring over the ground,
      Like a hunting-hound!
    For this is Thanksgiving Day.

Over the river and through the wood,
    And straight through the barnyard gate.
      We seem to go
      Extremely slow,—
    It is so hard to wait!

Over the river and through the wood—
    Now grandmother's cap I spy!
      Hurrah for the fun!
      Is the pudding done?
    Hurrah for the pumpkin-pie!

THE PUMPKIN

John Greenleaf Whittier

h! on Thanksgiving Day, when from East and from West,
From North and from South come the pilgrim and guest,
When the gray-haired New Englander sees round his board
The old broken links of affection restored,
When the care-wearied man seeks his mother once more,
And the worn matron smiles where the girl smiled before,
What moistens the lip and what brightens the eye?
What calls back the past, like the rich Pumpkin pie?
Oh—fruit loved of boyhood—the old days recalling,
When wood-grapes were purpling and brown nuts were falling!
When wild, ugly faces we carved in its skin,
Glaring out through the dark with a candle within!
When we laughed round the corn-heap, with hearts all in tune,
Our chair a broad pumpkin,—our lantern the moon,
Telling tales of a fairy who travelled like steam,
In a pumpkin-shell coach, with two rats for her team!

BIRCHES

Robert Frost

hen I see birches bend to left and right
Across the lines of straighter darker trees,
I like to think some boy's been swinging them.
But swinging doesn't bend them down to stay
As ice storms do. Often you must have seen them
Loaded with ice a sunny winter morning
After a rain. They click upon themselves
As the breeze rises, and turn many-colored
As the stir cracks and crazes their enamel.
Soon the sun's warmth makes them shed crystal shells
Shattering and avalanching on the snow crust—
Such heaps of broken glass to sweep away
You'd think the inner dome of heaven had fallen.

They are dragged to the withered bracken by the load,
And they seem not to break; though once they are bowed
So low for long, they never right themselves:
You may see their trunks arching in the woods
Years afterwards, trailing their leaves on the ground
Like girls on hands and knees that throw their hair
Before them over their heads to dry in the sun.
But I was going to say when Truth broke in
With all her matter of fact about the ice storm,
I should prefer to have some boy bend them
As he went out and in to fetch the cows—
Some boy too far from town to learn baseball,
Whose only play was what he found himself,
Summer or winter, and could play alone.
One by one he subdued his father's trees
By riding them down over and over again
Until he took the stiffness out of them,
And not one but hung limp, not one was left
For him to conquer. He learned all there was
To learn about not launching out too soon
And so not carrying the tree away
Clear to the ground. He always kept his poise
To the top branches, climbing carefully
With the same pains you use to fill a cup
Up to the brim, and even above the brim.
Then he flung outward, feet first, with a swish,
Kicking his way down through the air to the ground.
So was I once myself a swinger of birches.
And so I dream of going back to be.
It's when I'm weary of considerations,
And life is too much like a pathless wood
Where your face burns and tickles with the cobwebs
Broken across it, and one eye is weeping
From a twig's having lashed across it open.
I'd like to get away from earth awhile
And then come back to it and begin over.
May no fate willfully misunderstand me
And half grant what I wish and snatch me away
Not to return. Earth's the right place for love:
I don't know where it's likely to go better.
I'd like to go by climbing a birch tree,
And climb black branches up a snow-white trunk
Toward heaven, till the tree could bear no more,
But dipped its top and set me down again.
That would be good both going and coming back.
One could do worse than be a swinger of birches.

The Fox Hunt
Winslow Homer, 1893

CROWS

Valerie Worth

 hen the high
Snows lie worn
To rags along
The muddy furrows,

And the frozen
Sky frays, drooping
Gray and sodden
To the ground,

The sleek crows
Appear, flying
Low across the
Threadbare meadow

To jeer at
Winter's ruin
With their jubilant
Thaw, thaw, thaw!

FOX'S SONG

Barbara Angell

h bar arkh
a oo ooo a
na-hah na-hah na-hah
err arr arkh!
a oo ooo a

I trot lightly
like new snow
on delicate paws.
Moonsparks kindle
the fire of my pelt.

I sniff earth,
fungus, crumbling wood,
rabbits and small fur,
ruffle of chickens,
taste good blood.

I bark frosty answers
in the wooded night,
flow in and out of trees,
nip stars.

Ah bar arkh
a oo ooo a
na-hah na-hah na-hah
err arr arkh!
a oo ooo a

THE RAVEN

Edgar Allan Poe

Edgar Allan Poe
Mathew B. Brady, 1849

nce upon a midnight dreary, while I pondered, weak and weary,
Over many a quaint and curious volume of forgotten lore—
While I nodded, nearly napping, suddenly there came a tapping,
As of some one gently rapping, rapping at my chamber door.
"'Tis some visitor," I muttered, "tapping at my chamber door—
    Only this and nothing more."

Ah, distinctly I remember it was in the bleak December;
And each separate dying ember wrought its ghost upon the floor.
Eagerly I wished the morrow;—vainly I had sought to borrow
From my books surcease of sorrow—sorrow for the lost Lenore—
For the rare and radiant maiden whom the angels name Lenore—
    Nameless *here* for evermore.

And the silken, sad, uncertain rustling of each purple curtain
Thrilled me—filled me with fantastic terrors never felt before;
So that now, to still the beating of my heart, I stood repeating,
"'Tis some visitor entreating entrance at my chamber door—
Some late visitor entreating entrance at my chamber door;—
    This it is and nothing more."

Presently my soul grew stronger; hesitating then no longer,
"Sir," said I, "or Madam, truly your forgiveness I implore;
But the fact is I was napping, and so gently you came rapping,
And so faintly you came tapping, tapping at my chamber door,
That I scarce was sure I heard you"—here I opened wide the door;—
    Darkness there and nothing more.

Deep into that darkness peering, long I stood there wondering, fearing,
Doubting, dreaming dreams no mortal ever dared to dream before;
But the silence was unbroken, and the stillness gave no token,
And the only word there spoken was the whispered word, "Lenore?"
This I whispered, and an echo murmured back the word "Lenore!"
    Merely this and nothing more.

Back into the chamber turning, all my soul within me burning,
Soon again I heard a tapping somewhat louder than before.
"Surely," said I, "surely that is something at my window lattice;
Let me see, then, what thereat is, and this mystery explore—
Let my heart be still a moment and this mystery explore;—
    'Tis the wind and nothing more!"

Open here I flung the shutter, when, with many a flirt and flutter,
In there stepped a stately Raven of the saintly days of yore;
Not the least obeisance made he; not a minute stopped or stayed he;
But, with mien of lord or lady, perched above my chamber door—
Perched upon a bust of Pallas just above my chamber door—
    Perched, and sat, and nothing more.

Then this ebony bird beguiling my sad fancy into smiling,
By the grave and stern decorum of the countenance it wore,
"Though thy crest be shorn and shaven, thou," I said, "art sure no craven,
Ghastly grim and ancient Raven wandering from the Nightly shore—
Tell me what thy lordly name is on the Night's Plutonian shore!"
    Quoth the Raven, "Nevermore."

Much I marvelled this ungainly fowl to hear discourse so plainly,
Though its answer little meaning—little relevancy bore;
For we cannot help agreeing that no living human being
Ever yet was blessed with seeing bird above his chamber door—
Bird or beast upon the sculptured bust above his chamber door,
    With such name as "Nevermore."

But the Raven, sitting lonely on the placid bust spoke only
That one word, as if his soul in that one word he did outpour.
Nothing farther then he uttered—not a feather then he fluttered—
Till I scarcely more than muttered "Other friends have flown before—
On the morrow *he* will leave me, as my hopes have flown before."
    Then the bird said "Nevermore."

Startled at the stillness broken by reply so aptly spoken,
"Doubtless," said I, "what it utters is its only stock and store
Caught from some unhappy master whom unmerciful Disaster
Followed fast and followed faster till his songs one burden bore—
Till the dirges of his Hope that melancholy burden bore
    Of 'Never—nevermore.' "

But the Raven still beguiling all my fancy into smiling,
Straight I wheeled a cushioned seat in front of bird, and bust and door;
Then, upon the velvet sinking, I betook myself to linking
Fancy unto fancy, thinking what this ominous bird of yore—
What this grim, ungainly, ghastly, gaunt, and ominous bird of yore
    Meant in croaking "Nevermore."

This I sat engaged in guessing, but no syllable expressing
To the fowl whose fiery eyes now burned into my bosom's core;
This and more I sat divining, with my head at ease reclining
On the cushion's velvet lining that the lamp-light gloated o'er,
But whose velvet-violet lining with the lamp-light gloating o'er,
    She shall press, ah, nevermore!

Then, methought, the air grew denser, perfumed from an unseen censer
Swung by Seraphim whose foot-falls tinkled on the tufted floor.
"Wretch," I cried, "thy God hath lent thee—by these angels he hath sent thee
Respite—respite and nepenthe from thy memories of Lenore;
Quaff, oh, quaff this kind nepenthe and forget this lost Lenore!"
    Quoth the Raven, "Nevermore."

"Prophet!" said I, "thing of evil!—prophet still, if bird or devil!—
Whether Tempter sent, or whether tempest tossed thee here ashore,

Desolate yet all undaunted, on this desert land enchanted—
On this home by Horror haunted—tell me truly, I implore—
Is there—*is* there balm in Gilead?—tell me—tell me, I implore!"
    Quoth the Raven, "Nevermore."

"Prophet!" said I, "thing of evil!—prophet still, if bird or devil!
By that Heaven that bends above us—by that God we both adore—
Tell this soul with sorrow laden if, within the distant Aidenn,
It shall clasp a sainted maiden whom the angels name Lenore—
Clasp a rare and radiant maiden whom the angels name Lenore."
    Quoth the Raven, "Nevermore."

"Be that word our sign of parting, bird or fiend!" I shrieked, upstarting—
"Get thee back into the tempest and the Night's Plutonian shore!
Leave no black plume as a token of that lie thy soul hath spoken!
Leave my loneliness unbroken!—quit the bust above my door!
Take thy beak from out my heart, and take thy form from off my door!"
    Quoth the Raven, "Nevermore."

And the Raven, never flitting, still is sitting, *still* is sitting
On the pallid bust of Pallas just above my chamber door;
And his eyes have all the seeming of a demon's that is dreaming,
And the lamp-light o'er him streaming throws his shadow on the floor;
And my soul from out that shadow that lies floating on the floor
    Shall be lifted—nevermore!

STOPPING BY WOODS ON A SNOWY EVENING

Robert Frost

 hose woods these are I think I know.
His house is in the village, though;
He will not see me stopping here
To watch his woods fill up with snow.

My little horse must think it queer
To stop without a farmhouse near
Between the woods and frozen lake
The darkest evening of the year.

He gives his harness bells a shake
To ask if there is some mistake.
The only other sound's the sweep
Of easy wind and downy flake.

The woods are lovely, dark, and deep,
But I have promises to keep,
And miles to go before I sleep,
And miles to go before I sleep.

The Girl with the Dog
Theodore Robinson, about 1880

MY DOG

Marchette Chute

is nose is short and scrubby;
   His ears hang rather low;
And he always brings the stick back,
   No matter how far you throw.

He gets spanked rather often
   For things he shouldn't do,
Like lying-on-beds, and barking,
   And eating up shoes when they're new.

He always wants to be going
   Where he isn't supposed to go.
He tracks up the house when it's snowing—
   Oh, puppy, I love you so.

LULLABY

Robert Hillyer

The long canoe
Toward the shadowy shore,
One . . . two . . .
Three . . . four . . .
The paddle dips,
Turns in the wake,
Pauses, then
Forward again,
Water drips
From the blade to the lake.
Nothing but that,
No sound of wings;
The owl and bat
Are velvet things.
No wind awakes,
No fishes leap,
No rabbits creep
Among the brakes.

The long canoe
At the shadowy shore,
One . . . two . . .
Three . . . four . . .
A murmur now
Under the prow
Where rushes bow
To let us through.
One . . . two . . .
Upon the shore,
Three . . . four . . .
Upon the lake,
No one's awake,
No one's awake,
One . . .
Two . . .
No one,
Not even
You.

Twilight
Frank Benson, 1930

APRIL RAIN SONG

Langston Hughes

et the rain kiss you.
Let the rain beat upon your head with silver liquid drops.
Let the rain sing you a lullaby.

The rain makes still pools on the sidewalk.
The rain makes running pools in the gutter.
The rain plays a little sleep-song on our roof at night—

And I love the rain.

THE DARK AND FALLING SUMMER

Delmore Schwartz

he rain was full of the freshness
     and the fresh fragrance of darkening grapes.
The rain was as the dark falling of hidden
And fabulous plums ripening—great blue thunderheads
     moving slowly.
The dark air was possessed by the fragrance of freshness,
By a scattered and confused profusion until,
After the tattering began, the pouring-down came,
And plenitude descended, multitudinous.
Everywhere was full of the pulsing of the loud and fallen dusk.

SUNDAY AT THE END OF SUMMER

Howard Nemerov

ast night the cold wind and the rain blew
Hard from the west, all night, until the creek
Flooded, tearing the end of a wooden bridge
Down to hang, trembling, in the violent water.

This morning, with the weather still in rage,
I watched workmen already at repairs.
Some hundred of us came around to watch,
With collars turned against the rain and wind.

Down the wild water, where men stood to the knees,
We saw come flooding hollyhock and vine,
Sunflowers tall and broken, thorny bramble
And pale lilies cracked along the stalk.

Ours was the Sunday's perfect idleness
To watch those others working; who fought, swore,
Being threshed at hip and thigh, against that trash
Of pale wild flowers and their drifting legs.

Rainy Day on the Farm of Mr. Addison, Westfield, Connecticut
Jack Delano, 1940

WEATHER

hether the weather be fine
Or whether the weather be not,
Whether the weather be cold
Or whether the weather be hot,
We'll weather the weather
Whatever the weather,
Whether we like it or not.

THE LIGHTNING

May Swenson

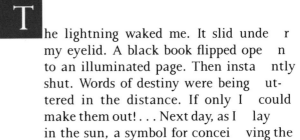
he lightning waked me. It slid under
my eyelid. A black book flipped open
to an illuminated page. Then instantly
shut. Words of destiny were being uttered in the distance. If only I could
make them out! . . . Next day, as I lay
in the sun, a symbol for conceiving the
universe was scratched on my eyeball.
But quickly its point eclipsed, and
softened, in the scabbard of my brain.

My cat speaks one word: Four vowels
and a consonant. He receives with the
hairs of his body the whispers of the
stars. The kinglet speaks by flashing
into view a ruby feather on his head.
He is held by a thread to the eye of
the sun and cannot fall into error.
Any flower is a perfect ear, or else it
is a thousand lips . . . When will I grope
clear of the entrails of intellect?

Modern Painting with Bolt
by Roy Lichtenstein, 1966

Patchwork Known as the "Gossips"
19th century

LISTEN!

Lilian Moore

Listen!
Listen to the witch!

grinch grinch grunch

chip-chop crunch

grickle

grackle

grooble

grobble

munch

munch

munch

Whatever in the world
is she having for lunch?

PATCHES OF SKY

Debora Greger

Like a map blanketing a bed,
the flat fields slope enough so
under snow at sunrise some are coral,
some cornflower—cartographer's tints
taken from an old quilt.

Four hawks revolve over the square
where the wind has hollowed out a house,
and the next one, where it fills a tree
with feathered leaves, beaked cries.
Or so I say. Expansive for once,

I want to show you a countryside,
not a bed. Look—low hills folding
over centuries and at their base
someone's ragged crocuses
in what must have been a garden,

a civilizing introduction of the frivolous
to dirt that supports not much but itself.
Think of the first tenants of this house,
two schoolteacher spinsters.
Did they wear red,

the intensity missing in the view?
What held them, sisters, together?
They slept, one on each side
of the double fireplace, under these quilts.
Look—the dark side of each square

is patched from a man's old suits,
the light from flowered dresses.
Did one of them ever feel like this,
asking who she belonged to,
the other answering, "Whom?"

MENDING WALL

Robert Frost

Something there is that doesn't love a wall,
That sends the frozen-ground-swell under it
And spills the upper boulders in the sun,
And makes gaps even two can pass abreast.
The work of hunters is another thing:
I have come after them and made repair
Where they have left not one stone on a stone,
But they would have the rabbit out of hiding,
To please the yelping dogs. The gaps I mean,
No one has seen them made or heard them made,
But at spring mending-time we find them there.
I let my neighbor know beyond the hill;
And on a day we meet to walk the line
And set the wall between us once again.
We keep the wall between us as we go.
To each the boulders that have fallen to each.
And some are loaves and some so nearly balls
We have to use a spell to make them balance:
"Stay where you are until our backs are turned!"
We wear our fingers rough with handling them.
Oh, just another kind of outdoor game,
One on a side. It comes to little more:
There where it is we do not need the wall:
He is all pine and I am apple orchard.
My apple trees will never get across
And eat the cones under his pines, I tell him.
He only says, "Good fences make good neighbors."
Spring is the mischief in me, and I wonder
If I could put a notion in his head:
"*Why* do they make good neighbors? Isn't it
Where there are cows? But here there are no cows.
Before I built a wall I'd ask to know
What I was walling in or walling out,
And to whom I was like to give offense.
Something there is that doesn't love a wall,
That wants it down." I could say "Elves" to him,
But it's not elves exactly, and I'd rather
He said it for himself. I see him there,
Bringing a stone grasped firmly by the top
In each hand, like an old-stone savage armed.
He moves in darkness as it seems to me,
Not of woods only and the shade of trees.
He will not go behind his father's saying,
And he likes having thought of it so well
He says again, "Good fences make good neighbors."

WHEN I MARRIED

from *Letter To My Mother*

John Holmes

hen I married, I caught up
On the history of the heart.
I stepped into your generation,
That welcoming fort,

That house you kept house in
While I was a child.
Now I am in my open door
Standing, and growing old.

Fond, and kind, and faithful
By a habit of the heart,
You keep with your own quiet
The world from falling apart.

But the world runs down, dust
Falls, the young become the old.
You learned that long ago,
And hold all you have held.

I am my father, and have a son.
Our voices sound the same.
Troubles we may not have alone
Are spelled in our name.

Your face was bone and width your own,
But half of yours is mine
To stare with at a world not wrong,
Not right, but by design

A clearing, a clouding tree of stars
That put down roots and grew.
I live under its shine and shade,
And can what I must do.

Dorothea and Francesca
Cecilia Beaux, 1898

Arrangement in Gray & Black:
The Artist's Mother
James McNeill Whistler, 1871

SLEEP, GRANDMOTHER

Mark Van Doren

leep, grandmother, sleep.
The rocking chair is ready to go,
And harness bells are hung in a row
As once you heard them
In soft snow.

Sleep, grandmother, sleep.
Your sons are little and silly again;
Your daughters are five and seven and ten;
And he that is gone
Was not gone then.

Sleep, grandmother, sleep.
The sleigh comes out of the winter woods
And carries you all in boots and hoods
To town for candy
And white dress goods.

Sleep, grandmother, sleep.
The rocking chair is old as the floor,
But there he nods, at the noisy door,
For you to be dancing
One dance more.

MY LOST YOUTH

Henry Wadsworth Longfellow

Often I think of the beautiful town
  That is seated by the sea,
Often in thought go up and down
The pleasant streets of that dear old town,
  And my youth comes back to me.
    And a verse of a Lapland song
    Is haunting my memory still:
  "A boy's will is the wind's will,
And the thoughts of youth are long, long thoughts."

I can see the shadowy lines of its trees,
  And catch, in sudden gleams,
The sheen of the far-surrounding seas,
And islands that were the Hesperides
  Of all my boyish dreams.
    And the burden of that old song,
    It murmurs and whispers still:
  "A boy's will is the wind's will,
And the thoughts of youth are long, long thoughts."

Gloucester Harbor and Dory
Winslow Homer, 1880

I remember the black wharves and the slips,
  And the sea-tides tossing free,
And Spanish sailors with bearded lips,
And the beauty and mystery of the ships,
  And the magic of the sea.
    And the voice of that wayward song
    Is singing and saying still:
  "A boy's will is the wind's will,
And the thoughts of youth are long, long thoughts."

I remember the bulwarks by the shore,
  And the fort upon the hill;
The sunrise gun, with its hollow roar,
The drum-beat repeated o'er and o'er,
  And the bugle wild and shrill.
    And the music of that old song
    Throbs in my memory still:
  "A boy's will is the wind's will,
And the thoughts of youth are long, long thoughts."

I remember the sea-fight far away,
  How it thundered o'er the tide!
And the dead captains, as they lay
In their graves, o'erlooking the tranquil bay,
  Where they in battle died.
    And the sound of that mournful song
    Goes through me with a thrill:
  "A boy's will is the wind's will,
And the thoughts of youth are long, long thoughts."

I can see the breezy dome of groves,
    The shadows of Deering's Woods;
And the friendships old and the early loves
Come back with a sabbath sound, as of doves
    In quiet neighborhoods.
        And the verse of that sweet old song,
        It flutters and murmurs still:
    "A boy's will is the wind's will,
And the thoughts of youth are long, long thoughts."

I remember the gleams and glooms that dart
    Across the school-boy's brain;
The song and the silence in the heart,
That in part are prophecies and in part
    Are longings wild and vain.
        And the voice of that fitful song
        Sings on, and is never still:
    "A boy's will is the wind's will,
And the thoughts of youth are long, long thoughts."

There are things of which I may not speak;
    There are dreams that cannot die;
There are thoughts that make the strong heart weak,
And bring a pallor into the cheek
    And a mist before the eye.
        And the words of that fatal song
        Come over me like a chill:
    "A boy's will is the wind's will,
And the thoughts of youth are long, long thoughts."

Strange to me now are the forms I meet
    When I visit the dear old town;
But the native air is pure and sweet,
And the trees that o'ershadow each well-known street
    As they balance up and down,
        Are singing the beautiful song,
        Are sighing and whispering still:
    "A boy's will is the wind's will,
And the thoughts of youth are long, long thoughts."

And Deering's Woods are fresh and fair;
    And with joy that is almost pain
My heart goes back to wander there,
And among the dreams of the days that were
    I find my lost youth again.
        And the strange and beautiful song,
        The groves are repeating it still:
    "A boy's will is the wind's will,
And the thoughts of youth are long, long thoughts."

Christina's World
Andrew Wyeth, 1948

SPRING

Marjorie Frost Fraser

o tangled grass I cling
When in the fields I lie,
For fear of taking wing.

When mountain torrents bring
The last of winter by,
To tangled grass I cling.

When maple tassles swing
Pure gold against the sky,
To tangled grass I cling.

Alighted robins sing
A song I dare not try
For fear of taking wing.

AFTERNOON ON A HILL

Edna St. Vincent Millay

 will be the gladdest thing
  Under the sun!
I will touch a hundred flowers
  And not pick one.

I will look at cliffs and clouds
  With quiet eyes,
Watch the wind bow down the grass,
  And the grass rise.

And when lights begin to show
  Up from the town,
I will mark which must be mine,
  And then start down!

The Open Air Breakfast
William Merritt Chase, about 1888

AND WHAT IS SO RARE AS A DAY IN JUNE

from *The Vision of Sir Launfal*

James Russell Lowell

And what is so rare as a day in June?
    Then, if ever, come perfect days;
Then Heaven tries earth if it be in tune,
    And over it softly her warm ear lays;
Whether we look, or whether we listen,
    We hear life murmur, or see it glisten;
Every clod feels a stir of might,
    An instinct within it that reaches and towers,
And, groping blindly above it for light,
    Climbs to a soul in grass and flowers.

THERE'S A CERTAIN SLANT OF LIGHT

Emily Dickinson

here's a certain slant of light,
On winter afternoons,
That oppresses, like the weight
Of cathedral tunes.

Heavenly hurt it gives us;
We can find no scar,
But internal difference
Where the meanings are.

None may teach it anything,
'Tis the seal, despair,—
An imperial affliction
Sent us of the air.

When it comes, the landscape listens,
Shadows hold their breath;
When it goes, 'tis like the distance
On the look of death.

MY LIFE CLOSED TWICE BEFORE ITS CLOSE

Emily Dickinson

y life closed twice before its close;
    It yet remains to see
If Immortality unveil
    A third event to me,

So huge, so hopeless to conceive,
    As these that twice befell.
Parting is all we know of heaven,
    And all we need of hell.

AUGUST

Celia Thaxter

Buttercup nodded and said good-by,
  Clover and daisy went off together,
But the fragrant water lilies lie
  Yet moored in the golden August weather.
The swallows chatter about their flight,
  The cricket chirps like a rare good fellow,
The asters twinkle in clusters bright,
  While the corn grows ripe and the apples mellow.

THE SANDPIPER

Celia Thaxter

Across the lonely beach we flit,
One little sandpiper and I,
And fast I gather, bit by bit,
The scattered drift-wood, bleached and dry.
The wild waves reach their hands for it,
The wild wind raves, the tide runs high,
As up and down the beach we flit,
One little sandpiper and I.

Above our heads the sullen clouds
Scud, black and swift, across the sky;
Like silent ghosts in misty shrouds
Stand out the white light-houses high.
Almost as far as eye can reach
I see the close-reefed vessels fly,
As fast we flit along the beach,
One little sandpiper and I.

I watch him as he skims along,
Uttering his sweet and mournful cry;
He starts not at my fitful song,
Nor flash of fluttering drapery.
He has no thought of any wrong,
He scans me with a fearless eye;
Stanch friends we are, well tried and strong,
The little sandpiper and I.

Shell
H. Landshoff

MAGGIE AND MILLY
AND MOLLY AND MAY

e. e. cummings

aggie and milly and molly and may
went down to the beach (to play one day)

and maggie discovered a shell that sang
so sweetly she couldn't remember her troubles, and

milly befriended a stranded star
whose rays five languid fingers were;

and molly was chased by a horrible thing
which raced sideways while blowing bubbles: and

may came home with a smooth round stone
as small as a world and as large as alone.

For whatever we lose (like a you or a me)
it's always ourselves we find in the sea

THE MORNS ARE MEEKER THAN THEY WERE

Emily Dickinson

The morns are meeker than they were,
    The nuts are getting brown;
The berry's cheek is plumper,
    The rose is out of town.

The maple wears a gayer scarf,
    The field a scarlet gown.
Lest I should be old-fashioned,
    I'll put a trinket on.

THE RED LEAF

Page Sullivan

That beautiful color on the leaf
    was once on a tree; it sat with
all the others.

    The edges are rippled and it has
    holes in it and soon it will be
no more, for autumn has come.

    The lines on the leaf help
    show off its beauty that is all
over it.

    I sit here admiring the leaf
    from all angles, watching it grow
redder and redder as my eyes
wander up the leaf.

Autumn Leaves, Lake George, N.Y.
Georgia O'Keeffe, 1924

Merry-Go-Round
Maurice Prendergast, 1900

CROSSING THE PARK

Howard Moss

 rossing the park to see a painting
Somebody painted of the park—
One that I once found more enchanting
Than the park itself—I stopped to look

At the cocksure pigeons, mincing on gravel,
The trees, each reading its own green book,
And felt the amphibian nerve and muscle
Of life quiver like a tuning fork,

Then steady itself to evoke some distant,
Wordless country existing still,
Growing louder on what was silent,
Its wild, sad energy visible

In hundreds of forms of pulsing shadow
Boned by the light, and then formed again
By the light—to the right, an imperfect meadow,
To the left, a sleeping, unfinished man—

Forms never to be composed so neatly,
Finished, framed, and set out to view
As the painting that hung in the nearby gallery
In permanent green, in abiding blue,

Central Park, 1901
Maurice Prendergast

For any vision must mean that something
Is being omitted; being discrete
By making the possible seem like one thing
Means lopping the head off or the feet,

Or leaving a leaf out or one wave
Of that merciless connoisseur, the sea,
Or pretending the body exists for love,
Or forgetting the pictures of misery

That are found in the news each day, that spell
Out fortunes each night across the sky:
The terrible kingdoms of the small,
The crystal ball of every eye.

The sun relinquished the sky. In slow
Inches the shade climbed up the trees.
Too late to get where I started to,
I watched their metamorphoses

Gradually give up the light
Till there was nothing more to give
To leaves and lives whose forms dispute
Those parks, those paintings in which I live.

I NEVER SAW A MOOR

Emily Dickinson

never saw a moor,
I never saw the sea;
Yet know I how the heather looks,
And what a wave must be.

I never spoke with God,
Nor visited in heaven;
Yet certain am I of the spot
As if the chart were given.

BECAUSE I COULD NOT STOP FOR DEATH

Emily Dickinson

ecause I could not stop for Death,
He kindly stopped for me;
The carriage held but just ourselves
And Immortality.

We slowly drove, he knew no haste,
And I had put away
My labor, and my leisure too,
For his civility.

We passed the school where children played
Their lessons scarcely done
We passed the fields of gazing grain,
We passed the setting sun.

We paused before a house that seemed
A swelling of the ground;
The roof was scarcely visible,
The cornice but a mound.

Since then 'tis centuries; but each
Feels shorter than the day
I first surmised the horses' heads
Were toward eternity.

Astronaut Sharon Christa McAulliffe

THE WORDS OF THE TRUE POEMS

Walt Whitman

The words of the true poems give you more than poems,
They give you to form for yourself poems, religions, politics, war,
      peace, behavior, histories, essays, daily life, and every thing else,
They balance ranks, colors, races, creeds, and the sexes,
They do not seek beauty, they are sought,
Forever touching them or close upon them follows beauty, longing, fain, love-sick.
They prepare for death, yet they are not the finish, but rather the outset,
They bring none to his or her terminus or to be content and full,
Whom they take they take into space to behold the birth of stars, to learn
      one of the meanings,
To launch off with absolute faith, to sweep through the ceaseless rings
      and never be quiet again.

List of Illustrations

Arts, Boston   Page 62. *Phillis Wheatley.* Artist unknown. After Scipio Moorhead. 1773. Engraving, 5¹/₁₆ x 4″. National Portrait Gallery, Smithsonian Institution. Published in Phillis Wheatley's *Poems on Various Subjects, Religious and Moral*   Page 64. *George Washington.* Gilbert Stuart. 1796. Oil on canvas, 48 x 37″. Jointly owned by the Museum of Fine Arts, Boston, and the National Portrait Gallery, Washington, D.C.   Page 65. Workmen completing the Washington Monument. Photographer unknown. 1884. Library of Congress   Page 66. *John Paul Jones.* Revolutionary War naval officer, after Jean-Antoine Houdon. c. 1780s. Bronze, cast after 1780 plaster, height 27¹/₄″. National Portrait Gallery, Smithsonian Institution   Page 67. *Battle Between John Paul Jones's* Bonhomme Richard *and Richard Pearson's* Serapis. B. F. Leizalt. c. 1781. Etching, after a drawing by Richard Paton. Library of Congress   Page 68. *Walt Whitman with Nigel and Catherine Jeanette Cholmeley-Jones.* George Collins Cox. c. 1887 (attributed). Silver print, 9¹/₄ x 7³/₄″. Division of Photographic History, Smithsonian Institution   Page 69. *Abraham Lincoln Reading with his son Tad.* Photograph by Mathew B. Brady. 1860s. Library of Congress   Page 70. Watercolor rendering by E. Boyd of a chest showing Spanish dancers and cowboy. c. 1820, made in New Mexico. Chest is pine painted in oil. Index of American Design, National Gallery of Art, Washington, D.C.   Page 71. *Over the River to Grandmother's House.* Grandma Moses. 1945. Oil on masonite, 45 x 75 cm. © 1987, Grandma Moses Properties Company, New York   Page 74. *The Fox Hunt.* Winslow Homer. 1893. Oil on canvas, 38 x 68¹/₂″. The Pennsylvania Academy of the Fine Arts, Philadelphia, Temple Fund Purchase   Page 76. *Edgar Allan Poe.* Photograph by Mathew B. Brady. 1849. Library of Congress   Page 79. *The Girl with the Dog.* Theodore Robinson. c. 1880. Oil on canvas, 19¹/₄ x 13¹/₄″. Cincinnati Art Museum, Gift of Mrs. A. M. Adler. Accession #1970. 751   Page 81. *Twilight.* Frank Benson, 1930. Oil on canvas, 40 x 50″. Giussepe Waltoni Collection, Boston   Page 83. *Rainy Day on the Farm of Mr. Addison, Westfield, Connecticut.* Photograph by Jack Delano. 1940. Library of Congress   Page 85. *Modern Painting with Bolt.* Roy Lichtenstein. 1966. Synthetic polymer paint and oil partly silkscreened on canvas, 66¹/₄ x 68³/₈″.

© Roy Lichtenstein. Collection, The Museum of Modern Art, New York. The Sidney and Harriet Janis Collection.   Page 86. Watercolor rendering by Carmel Wilson of a Patchwork known as the "Gossips." 19th century, made in Vermont. Folk art object, silk appliqué. Index of American Design, National Gallery of Art, Washington, D.C.   Page 88. *Dorothea and Francesca.* Cecilia Beaux. 1898. Oil on canvas, 80¹/₈ x 46″. © 1988 The Art Institute of Chicago, A. A. Munger Collection, 1921.109   Page 89. *Arrangement in Gray and Black: The Artist's Mother.* James McNeill Whistler. 1871. Oil, 57 x 64¹/₂″. Collection, Le Louvre, Paris (photo: Service Photographique des Musées Nationaux, Paris)   Page 91. *Gloucester Harbor and Dory.* Winslow Homer. 1880. Watercolor, 13¹/₄ x 19″. Fogg Art Museum, Anonymous Gift (photo: courtesy of the Harvard University Art Museums, Cambridge)   Page 92. *Christina's World.* Andrew Wyeth. 1948. Tempera on gesso panel, 32¹/₄ x 47³/₄″. Collection, The Museum of Modern Art, New York. Purchase   Page 93. *The Open Air Breakfast.* William Merritt Chase. c. 1888. Oil on canvas, 37⁷/₁₆ x 56³/₄″. Gift of Florence Scott Libbey. The Toledo Museum of Art (53.136)   Page 95. *Emily Dickinson.* Photographer unknown. 19th century. Height 2⁹/₁₆, width 2¹/₁₆″. By permission of the Houghton Library, Harvard University. Emily Dickinson Collection   Page 96. *Mary Beekman, About Two Years Old, with Pet Lamb.* John Durand. 1766. Oil. Collection, The New-York Historical Society   Page 97. *Cow Triptych.* Roy Lichtenstein. 1974. Oil and magna on canvas, 3 panels, ea. 68 x 62″. © Roy Lichtenstein (photo: courtesy Leo Castelli Gallery, New York)   Page 99. Shell. Photograph by H. Landshoff   Page 101. *Autumn Leaves, Lake George, N.Y.* Georgia O'Keeffe. 1924. Oil on canvas, 20¹/₄ x 16¹/₄″. Columbus Museum of Art, Ohio: Museum Purchase, Howald Fund II. Copyright 1978 Estate of Georgia O'Keeffe   Page 102. *Merry-Go-Round.* Maurice Prendergast. Pencil and watercolor, 13¹/₄″ x 19″. Museum of Fine Arts, Springfield, Massachusetts   Page 103. *Central Park, 1901.* Maurice Prendergast. 1901. Watercolor on paper, 14³/₈ x 21¹/₂″. Collection of Whitney Museum of American Art. Purchase. 32.42 (photo: Gamma One Conversions Inc., New York)   Page 105. Astronaut Sharon Christa McAulliffe. Photograph by NASA, Washington, D.C.

Acknowledgments

Grateful acknowledgment is made for permission to reproduce the following poems. All possible care has been taken to trace ownership of every selection included and to make full acknowledgment. If any errors or omissions have occurred, they will be corrected in subsequent editions, provided notification is sent to the publisher.

"Fox's Song" by Barbara Angell, from *Games & Puzzles*, Cleveland State University Poetry Center. Copyright © 1978 by Barbara Angell.

"Western Wagons" by Rosemary and Stephen Vincent Benét, from *The Selected Works of Stephen Vincent Benét*, Holt, Rinehart and Winston, Inc. Copyright 1937 by Stephen Vincent Benét. Copyright renewed © 1964 by Thomas Benét, Stephanie B. Manin and Rachel Benét Lewis. Reprinted by permission of Brandt & Brandt Literary Agents, Inc.

"Ruby Dear" lyrics by David Byrne and music by David Byrne, Jerry Harrison, Chris Frantz, and Tina Weymouth. © 1988, Index Music Inc. (ASCAP).

"My Dog" by Marchette Chute, from *Around and About*, E. P. Dutton, Inc. Copyright 1957 by E. P. Dutton, Inc. Copyright renewed 1985 by Marchette Chute. Reprinted by permission of the author.

"Magic Words" from *Songs and Stories of the Netsilik Eskimos*, translated by Edward Fields from text collected by Knud Rasmussen, courtesy Education Development Center, Inc., Newton, MA.

"Sleep, Grandmother" by Mark Van Doren, from *Collected and New Poems*. Copyright 1963 by Mark Van Doren. "Crows" by Valerie Worth, from *Small Poems Again*. Copyright 1975, 1986 by Valerie Worth. Reprinted by permission of Farrar, Straus and Giroux, Inc.

"Spring" by Marjorie Frost Fraser. Permission courtesy of the family.

"The Song of the Jellicles" by T. S. Eliot, from *Old Possum's Book of Practical Cats*. Copyright 1939 by T. S. Eliot, renewed 1967 by Esme Valerie Eliot. "Skyscraper" by Carl Sandburg, from *Chicago Poems*. Copyright 1916 by Holt, Rinehart and Winston, Inc., renewed 1944 by Carl Sandburg. "There are Different Gardens" and "Milk-White Moon, Put the Cows to Sleep" by Carl Sandburg, from *Good Morning America*. Copyright 1928, 1956 by Carl Sandburg. "Washington Monument by Night" by Carl Sandburg, from *Slabs of the Sunburnt West*. Copyright 1922 by Harcourt Brace Jovanovich, Inc., renewed 1950 by Carl Sandburg. "The Writer" by Richard Wilbur, from *The Mind-Reader: New Poems*. Copyright © 1955, 1971 by Richard Wilbur, originally published in *The New Republic*. "Digging for China" by Richard Wilbur, from *Things of This World*. Copyright © 1956, 1984 by Richard Wilbur. All reprinted by permission of Harcourt Brace Jovanovich, Inc.

"Rock 'N' Roll Band" by Shel Silverstein, from *A Light in the Attic*. "Schoolcraft's Diary Written on the Missouri: 1830" by Robert Bly, from *Selected Poems*. Copyright 1986 by Robert Bly. Reprinted by permission of Harper & Row, Publishers, Inc.

"Warrior Nation Trilogy" by Lance Henson, from *Voices of the Rainbow*, Viking, 1975. Copyright by Lance Henson.

"Boy Reading" and "Metaphor for my Son" by John Holmes, from *Map of My Country*, Duell, Sloan and Pearce, 1943. Copyright © 1943 by John Holmes. "When I Married" excerpt from "Letter to My Mother" by John Holmes, from *The Fortune Teller*, Harper & Brothers, 1961. Copyright © 1961 by John Holmes. Reprinted by permission of Doris Holmes Eyges.

"Birches," "Mending Wall," "The Telephone," and "Stopping by Woods on a Snowy Evening" by Robert Frost, from *The Poetry of Robert Frost*, edited by Edward Connery Lathem. Copyright © 1969 by Holt, Rinehart and Winston, Inc. Copyright © 1962 by Robert Frost. Copyright © 1975 by Lesley Frost Ballantine. Reprinted by permission of Henry Holt and Company, Inc.

"A Song of Greatness" transcribed by Mary Austin, from *The Children Sing In the Far West*. Copyright © 1928 by Mary Austin. Copyright © renewed 1956 by Kenneth M. Chapman and Mary C. Wheelwright. Reprinted by permission of Houghton Mifflin Company.

"High Flight" by John Gillespie Magee, Jr., from the *New York Herald Tribune*, February 8, 1942. Courtesy I. H. T. Corporation.

"Theatre Hour" by Ogden Nash, from *Everyone But Thee and Me*. Copyright © 1962 by Ogden Nash. Copyright © renewed 1986 by Frances Nash, Isabel Nash Eberstadt, and Linnell Nash Smith. "Eletelephony" by Laura E. Richards, from *Tirra-Lirra: Rhymes Old and New*. Copyright © 1930, 1932 by Laura E. Richards. Copyright © renewed 1960 by Hamilton Richards. By permission of Little, Brown and Company.

"maggie and milly and molly and may" by e. e. cummings, from *Complete Poems, 1913-1962*. Copyright © 1923, 1925, 1931, 1935, 1938-40, 1944-62 by the Trustees for the E. E. Cummings Trust. Copyright © 1961, 1963, 1968 by Marion Morehouse Cummings. By permission of Liveright Publishing Corporation.

"Poetry" by Marianne Moore, from *Complete Poems*. Copyright 1935 by Marianne Moore, renewed 1963 by Marianne Moore and T. S. Eliot. "The Sheaves" by Edwin Arlington Robinson, from *Collected Poems*. Copyright 1925 by Edwin Arlington Robinson, renewed 1953 by Ruth Nivison and Barbara R. Holt. Reprinted with permission of Macmillan Publishing Company. "Crossing the Park" by Howard Moss, from *New Selected Poems*. Copyright © Howard Moss 1963. Originally appeared in *The New Yorker*. Reprinted with permission of Atheneum Publishers, an imprint of Macmillan Publishing Company.

"Afternoon on a Hill" by Edna St. Vincent Millay, from *Collected Poems*, Harper & Row. Copyright 1917, 1945 by Edna St. Vincent Millay. Reprinted by permission.

Poetry Title and Author Index